Escaping the Stress Trap

MARY SOUTHERLAND

HARVEST HOUSE PUBLISHERS

EUGENE, OREGON

Cover by Left Coast Design, Portland, Oregon

Cover photo © Glen Wexler / Masterfile

Every effort has been made to give proper credit for all stories, poems, and quotations. If for any reason proper credit has not been given, please notify the author or publisher and proper notation will be given on future printing.

Word studies are taken from the Hebrew-Greek Key Study Bible, Dr. Spiros Zodhiates, editor, copyright © 1996 by AMG International, Inc. Used by permission.

ESCAPING THE STRESS TRAP
Copyright © 2006 by Mary Southerland
Published by Harvest House Publishers
Eugene, Oregon 97402
www.harvesthousepublishers.com

Library of Congress Cataloging-in-Publication Data

Southerland, Mary.
   Escaping the stress trap / Mary Southerland.
      p. cm.
   ISBN-13: 978-0-7369-1816-9 (pbk.)
   ISBN-10: 0-7369-1816-7 (pbk.)
   1. Bible. O.T. Psalms XXIII--Criticism, interpretation, etc. 2. Stress management--Religious aspects--Christianity. 3. Time management--Religious aspects--Christianity. I. Title.
   BS145023rd .S68 2006
   248.8'6--dc22
                                    2006012307

Printed in the United States of America

06 07 08 09 10 11 12 13 14 / BP-SK / 10 9 8 7 6 5 4 3 2 1

This book is dedicated to...

The broken lamb in search of healing

The weary shepherd in need of rest

The chaotic heart crying out for peace

The desperate soul in search of a Savior

He has come.

O O O

For to us a child is born,

to us a son is given,

and the government will be on his shoulders.

And he will be called

Wonderful Counselor, Mighty God,

Everlasting Father, Prince of Peace.

ISAIAH 9:6

Acknowledgments

The first person I want to thank is my husband and best friend of 30 years, Dan. You continually carved out chunks of time, making it possible for me to write this book. You encouraged me to keep going when I wanted to give up. And during the bombardment of stressful situations, you loved me and walked with me through each one. I absolutely adore you!

I also want to thank our awesome children, Jered and Danna. Your understanding and patience during the writing of this particular book was amazing. I love you both so much!

Thanks to the Journey Ministry prayer warriors and members of Next Level Church. You have literally prayed me through every step of writing this book. You made me laugh when I felt like crying and spoke words of peace during the most stressful moments.

A special thanks to all of the Journey friends who submitted tips for dealing with stress. Your ideas will bless many and put feet to the truths of stress management.

Ellen and Sally, your content on nutrition and health is such an important contribution to this book. Thank you for sharing your wisdom!

Above all, thank You, God, my Shepherd, for being all I need for every stress-filled moment of life. You have filled my heart with peace and taught me to trust You for the next step, even when the path seems uncertain and the solution makes no sense. I praise You for guiding me through each valley and hammering down every mountain standing in my way. Thank You for allowing me to serve You. Thank You for Your peace that really does pass all human understanding. You are enough!

Contents

○ ○ ○

God, Help Me!

God, help me to relax about insignificant details,
beginning tomorrow at 7:41:23 AM EST.

God, help me to consider people's feelings,
even if most of them *are* hypersensitive.

God, help me to take responsibility for my own actions,
even though they are usually *not* my fault.

God, help me not to try to run everything,
but if You need my help, please feel free to ask.

God, help me to be more laid-back,
and help me to do it *exactly right*.

God, help me to take things more seriously,
especially laughter, parties, and dancing.

God, give me patience,
and I need it *now*.

God, help me not be a perfectionist.
(Did I write that correctly?)

God, help me to finish everything that I sta...

Amen!

AUTHOR UNKNOWN

As You Begin...

The LORD is my shepherd; I shall not want. He makes me to lie down in green pastures; He leads me beside the still waters. He restores my soul; He leads me in the paths of righteousness for His name's sake. Yea, though I walk through the valley of the shadow of death, I will fear no evil; for You are with me; Your rod and Your staff, they comfort me. You prepare a table before me in the presence of my enemies; You anoint my head with oil; My cup runs over. Surely goodness and mercy shall follow me all the days of my life; and I will dwell in the house of the LORD Forever.
PSALM 23 NKJV

While waiting for a red light to change, I noticed a bumper sticker on the car in front of me. "Just when I thought I was winning the rat race, along came faster rats!" I could so relate. My thoughts immediately drifted to the absurd schedule I had hurled myself through that day. It was a schedule without margins or boundaries. Every moment was assigned to something or someone. My stress level had grown with every task, threatening to overwhelm my heart and soul in a torrential emotional downpour of anxiety, tension, and stress. My head was pounding and my stomach was churning. I couldn't wait to get home, change into my comfort clothes, and escape to a quiet place of solitude and rest.

Stress, however, was eagerly awaiting my arrival at home. Children needed clean clothes, clamored for hot food, required transportation to various activities, begged for help with homework, and longed for a listening ear and the loving attention of a mother's heart. Right! I was ready to hand them off to my husband. But my husband, the pastor of a large and fast-growing church, had experienced the same kind of chaotic day I had lived through. He was also in desperate need of peace and quiet for his own frazzled soul.

I needed help, but I was certainly not alone in my desperation. Everywhere I looked and every person who crossed my path seemed to be fighting the same fight when it came to dealing with stress.

Stress is a familiar and faithful companion, an unavoidable part of life common to us all. It does not matter where our day takes us, we *will* encounter stress. We can neither run from nor avoid it. And, unless we learn how to manage and deal with that stress God's way, we will surely find ourselves trapped and become an easy target for the enemy.

A friend recently told me the story of a farmer who, as the owner of a large piece of land along the Atlantic seacoast, constantly advertised for hired hands. Most people were reluctant to work on farms along the Atlantic because of the terrible storms known to plague the area, destroying buildings and crops. As the farmer interviewed applicants, he received a steady stream of refusals. Finally, a short, thin man, well past middle age, approached the farmer, seeking employment. "Are you a good farm hand?" the farmer asked him. "Well, I can sleep when the wind blows," answered the little man. Although puzzled by this answer, the farmer, desperate for help, hired him.

The slight man worked hard around the farm, busy from morning 'til night. The farmer was delighted with the man's work. Then one night the wind howled as it blew in from offshore, signaling the approach of a monstrous storm. Jumping out of bed, the farmer grabbed a lantern and rushed next door to the hired hand's sleeping quarters. He shook the little man and yelled, "Get up! A storm is coming! Tie things down before they blow away!" The man rolled over in bed and firmly responded, "No, sir! I told you, I can sleep when the wind blows." Enraged by the seemingly impertinent response, the farmer was tempted to fire him on the spot. Instead, he hurried outside to prepare for the storm. To his amazement, he discovered that all of the haystacks had been covered with tarps. The cows were in the barn, the chickens were in their coops, the doors were barred, and the shutters were tightly secured. Everything was tied down. Nothing could blow away. The farmer then understood what his hired hand had meant. He returned to his bed to also sleep while the wind blew.

Stress management is a spiritual discipline that begins with diligent preparation in every area of life—mental, emotional, physical, and spiritual. We must be *ready* to deal with stress before we are *required* to deal with stress. Dealing with stress is an ongoing, daily battle that will not end this side of heaven. In order to win that battle, we must be prepared. While there is no single secret to handling stress, God's Word is filled with many truths that can enable and empower us to deal with stress in a healthy, productive and God-honoring way.

Sometimes the most familiar passages of Scripture are also the most overlooked. Psalm 23 is one of those passages. I often find myself going to this psalm for peace and comfort in the aftermath of a stressful situation or for guidance and shelter from the storm that I see barreling straight for the unprepared shores of my life. However, I have also discovered that Psalm 23 is a powerful tool for dealing with stress on an everyday basis.

If you are like me, I tend to handle major calamities better than the mundane, ordinary, but definitely stress-inducing minutia of daily living. A study of Psalm 23 has led me to believe that it's often the small pebble in my shoe, rather than the massive boulder on my path, that causes the greatest stress in my life. Life is so daily! Fortunately, so is God.

God delivered a profound message when He sent His Son, Jesus Christ, to live among us. Jesus could have come to us in many ways, but He chose to interrupt the ordinary with the extraordinary. Jesus could rightfully have been born in a palace. He was, after all, a King. Yet His life on earth began in a manger—a smelly, dusty, dirty, and definitely common place. The simplicity of His birth is one of His most precious gifts to us and a constant reminder that He really does care about everything that touches our lives—no matter how small or insignificant it may seem. God wants to be involved in the simple, ordinary happenings of each day.

While I cannot imagine my world without the presence and power of Jesus Christ, I'm often guilty of living as if He doesn't exist. The result is a stress-filled life. A trial comes and I try to handle it on my own. Loneliness empties my heart and, instead of reaching out to Him, I withdraw into the darkness where stress lurks, just waiting to fill that emptiness with anxiety and fear. Still, God is faithful. His peace is a soothing balm that leads me once again to the manger and away from stress. Emmanuel, God with *me!* He steps into my life and changes everything. When He comes, stress is stripped away and tranquility is given in its place.

When I find myself wishing I could have been there that holy night when Jesus was born, He gently reminds me that I had my own manger experience, when God became a personal reality in my life. I have my own holy moments each and every day as I reach out to Him and He is there, right in the middle of my common and often smelly circumstances.

Stress has no place in a heart that kneels before the manger. Stress is powerless in a life that continually seeks God and chooses to surrender to His love and care the way the sheep surrender to the love and care of their shepherd. Psalm 23 describes the intimate, personal, and trusting relationship between sheep and shepherd, between child and father, and it is not only a beautiful portrait of

God's complete and faithful provision, but also an arsenal of stress-busting truths and principles that, when embraced and applied, will empower and equip us to live a life of peace and victory.

Stress-Busters

- Take deep, slow breaths instead of the shallow, fast breaths stress generates. Sit up straight, feet flat on the floor. Breathe deeply, allowing your abdomen to expand. Slowly exhale. Repeat five times. A slower breathing rate reduces stress.

- Tensing and then relaxing muscle groups is a great stress-buster. Start with your neck and shoulders, then your shoulder blades, your forehead, and eyes. Inhale as you tense and exhale as you relax.

- Headaches, stomach discomfort, tense muscles, and restless sleep may be early indicators of too much stress. When you feel stress coming on, take a deep breath, pray, and surrender the stressful circumstance(s) to God.

- In stressful times, speak more slowly than usual. Stressed people tend to speak quickly. By slowing down your speech, you'll buy time to think more clearly while appearing less anxious and more in control of the situation.

- Choose one simple thing you have been putting off (returning a phone call, making a doctor's appointment) and do it immediately. Just taking care of one responsibility hanging over your head is energizing, can improve your attitude, and reduce stress.

- Sometimes just a change of scenery brings fresh perspective to stress-filled situations. Take a drive. While driving, listen to calming music or sing some of your stress away by tuning into your favorite station and belting out a song.

- Stop gritting your teeth. Stress tends to settle in certain parts of our bodies, the jaw being one of them. When things get hectic, place your index fingertips on your jaw joints, just in front of your ears; clench your teeth and inhale deeply. Hold the breath for a moment, and as you exhale say, "Ah-h-h-h," unclench your teeth. Repeat a few times.

- Briskly rub your hands together until they feel warm. Then cup them over your closed eyes for five seconds while you breathe deeply. The warmth and darkness are comforting.

- Stand or sit, stretch your arms out from your sides, and shake your hands vigorously for about ten seconds.

- When people are under stress, they tend to slump over as if carrying a burden. Doctors say that slumping restricts breathing and reduces blood and oxygen flow to the brain, increasing muscle tension and feelings of panic and helplessness. Straightening your spine has just the opposite effect. It promotes circulation, increases oxygen levels in your blood, and helps lessen muscle tension, all of which promote relaxation and reduce stress.

- When shopping for a particular item, call ahead to save time, unnecessary trips, and frustration.

- Give in occasionally. Give yourself a break. You don't always have to be right. Be flexible. Be willing to compromise. If you do, others may meet you halfway. If you know you are right, stand your ground, but be calm and rational.

1

Know Whose You Are

The LORD is my shepherd.
PSALM 23:1 NKJV

Jehovah-Raah: *The Lord My Shepherd*

~ The Shepherd and His Sheep ~

Shepherding is one of the oldest callings in Israel, even more than farming. Shepherds traveled from place to place, living in tents while driving their flocks from one pasture to another. The sheep and their shepherds lived together every minute of every day. In fact, they were so intimately bound together that individual sheep, even when mixed with other flocks, could recognize the voice of their own shepherd and would come immediately when called by name. A shepherd owned and marked his sheep. In some cases, the sheep were even branded, although branding is no longer an accepted method of identification because of the damage it does to the wool. Today, the ears of sheep are pierced with identification tags, but for thousands of years shepherds around the world marked their sheep by notching their ears with a sharp knife. Each shepherd had his own distinctive notch that indicated identity and ownership.

○ ○ ○

Learning to deal with stress begins with a vital, personal relationship with the forever-faithful, peace-giving, stress-busting God. An understanding of *who* we are and *whose* we are empowers us to live a life marked by peace—a life where the control and management of stress is consigned to the authority of God alone. It sounds simple, but it rarely is. The truth is that we are often blind to His unconditional love, unfettered acceptance of us, and total pleasure in who we are. My husband, Dan, understands the aggravation of struggling with sight:

> Eyesight has always been a frustration for me. As far back as first grade, I can remember being unable to see the blackboard unless I sat in the front row. Because I loved to talk, you can imagine that the front row was not my favorite place to sit. After two years of frustration, my parents took me to an optometrist, who promptly pronounced me "blind as a bat." From that moment on, glasses and/or contacts have been part of my daily routine.
>
> My first pair of glasses were nasty. Multicolored shades of brown, coke-bottle lenses, and the nickname "Four-Eyes" all came in one ugly package. But I could see—and that helped! I wore those glasses through Scouts and football, enduring the taunting that came with them. They became part of my every waking minute. In the ninth grade, I was doing well in football. Contacts were still a couple of years away from being available to the masses, so I wore glasses underneath my helmet, using an elastic strap to keep them in place. I was one mean All-District defensive end! I even played some fullback until the coach made a decision at the

start of the season: No glasses under the helmet. A Dallas football player had managed to cut his nose when his glasses were smashed during a game. My coach heard about it and declared he would not allow that to happen on his squad. So I lost my specs. I lost a great deal more than just a pair of glasses. I lost my ability to see—and, therefore, the ability to play with confidence. I was so blind that I could not see the play developing until it was right on top of me. After losing my starting job, I eventually lost interest and quit playing football altogether. As a college freshman, I found new eyesight life when I received my first pair of hard contact lenses. I loved them and wore them until an infection in my eyes took them away. I went back to wearing thick glasses. Several years later soft contacts came along, and once again my sight was reborn! I wore them every waking hour and was thrilled to be free of the nasty thick lenses I had worn for 20 plus years. However, my eyes then began to bother me whenever I wore my contacts. I tried new pairs, new prescriptions, and new types of soft lenses. All of them irritated my eyes. I went back to glasses: a smaller, not quite so thick pair, but still with all the hassles that wearing glasses brings. Once again, I had to lay them in the right spot in hotel rooms or at home every night because I literally could not see well enough to find them. By this time, my vision had deteriorated to 20/525 in each eye. I simply resigned myself to wearing glasses and went on with life. Maybe someday—post-college-tuition payments—I would be able to afford Lasik eye surgery.

Then I received a priceless gift! My best friend had Lasik surgery and was so thrilled with the results that he wanted me to have the same procedure and generously insisted on paying for it. The surgery went well and the results seemed promising. I slept through the first day, compliments of surgical sedation. But when I woke the next morning—I could see! I could see the time on my alarm clock, the trees outside my bedroom window—everything! I literally walked around the house, overwhelmed at my new world! I had new sight!

Spiritual sight is much the same. In John 9:25 we find the disciple's ecstatic proclamation, "I was blind but now I can see!" Like John, we are blind, trapped in a dark prison of ignorance, fear, and sin. Life is meaningless, without purpose, and the perfect setting for stress to reign. We long for freedom and light, frantically trying every human remedy for the terminal case of spiritual blindness with which we are all born. The only remedy, the only solution for that spiritual blindness, is found in a personal relationship with God. When we turn from the sin in our lives, choosing to commit ourselves wholly to Him, His presence replaces darkness with light, guilt with forgiveness, blindness with sight, and stress with peace. That personal relationship begins with our acknowledgment and acceptance of the truth that God knows us.

God Knows Me

To think that I can know God is, without a doubt, one of the most amazing truths in life, a truth I find humanly impossible to understand and difficult to grasp. However, to think that God knows *me* is a reality that absolutely rocks my world! But He really does. God knows me and is aware of my every thought, hears every word I speak, and delights in who I am.

Dan and I lived and ministered in South Florida for more than 20 years. Consequently, we rarely went anywhere without running into someone we knew. At times, the fact that we were well-known in the area was irritating, but for the most part, we enjoyed the wide circle of friends God gave us in ministry. Four years ago, we moved to North Carolina to begin the next chapter of our life and ministry. Dan started traveling full-time, training pastors and church leaders around the world. Our son, Jered, graduated from high school and went away to college—which left me at home with Danna, our

16-year-old daughter. It was not a good thing! Looking back, however, it was actually the best thing for both of us.

Danna had absolutely no desire to leave South Florida, and she made it very clear that she was not happy with us for forcing her to move from her place of birth, the land of the free, where every friend she would ever have in her entire life lived! Danna has never been short on drama. "Whoever heard of living next to cows and goats? And why would anyone want to live in the mountains when they could live at the beach?" she wailed. I loved the mild winters. Not Danna. "I am going to freeze to death and then you'll be sorry," she promised. I found the friendliness of the people refreshing. "They are just nosy, Mom. You had better hang on to your purse and keep every door locked." The open spaces of North Carolina were a wonderful change from the cramped and crowded South Florida terrain. "It takes *forever* to get anywhere," Danna would moan as we drove 20 minutes to the nearest grocery store. Heaven help the country gentleman who dared to open a door for us! Danna would glare at him as if he were a stalker in search of his next victim. The soft Southern accents I enjoyed sent Danna into her best impersonation of "a Carolina redneck," twang dripping from every syllable of every word. "Seriously, Mom, who talks like that?" she would ask. In retrospect, it is a wonder either one of us is still alive.

I thought Danna's greatest struggle in moving to North Carolina was the fact that she didn't know anyone in this foreign land to which she had been exiled by her obviously misinformed and misguided parents. However, over dinner one night, she corrected my faulty perspective. "Danna, I know it's hard to start over in a place where you don't know anyone—" I began. Her instantaneous response caught me off guard. "Mom, it's *not* that I don't know anyone. The problem is that they don't know *me!*"

In that moment I realized that all of us define happiness and contentment on the basis of who cares that we are alive or is even aware that we exist. Stress is often the result of a relentless effort to be known. We garner worth and value by seeing ourselves in the eyes of others instead of seeing ourselves in the eyes of God. Just as a shepherd knows every sheep by name, God knows us.

When I met Dan Southerland, I immediately liked him and wanted to know more about him. As we worked together in youth ministry, a special friendship developed between us that deepened over the years and eventually led to our marriage. Not only have Dan and I been married 30 years, but we have served together in ministry during each one of those years. I can honestly say that I love him more today than I ever have. I know him. I can tell you Dan's opinions on most subjects without asking him. I know his habits, his fears, his likes, his dislikes, and his dreams, and at times I can even tell what he's thinking just by looking into his eyes.

I have a unique philosophy about my hair. I believe one of the reasons it exists atop my head is to provide a conduit for change and adventure in life. You might say that my hair is in a constant state of transition and experimentation. I've been known to tear a picture out of a catalog, thrust that picture into my hairstylist's hands, and command, "Make my hair look like this!" Other times I opt for a new color…or two…a different style or length…you get the idea. When I am feeling especially brave, I might walk into a brand-new salon, ask for the most experienced stylist available, plop into his or her chair, and simply hope for the best. Personally, I consider my "hair attitude" an ongoing exercise in faith, but you can probably understand why Dan tends to shudder when he hears me utter these fateful words, "Honey, I'll be back in a little while. I am going to get my hair done." Honestly, the way I wear my hair really is a minor issue to my sweet husband. Thank goodness! While running errands one day, Dan and I were enjoying the opportunity to catch up on life. During a lull in the conversation, I looked over to see him watching me with a mysterious smile on his face. "I know," I said. "I don't like it this way, either." Dan nearly wrecked the car! "What?" he sputtered. I grinned and explained, "I know you don't like my hair this way and I don't, either." He shook his head in amazement.

"But I did not say one word about your hair." With a knowing smile I responded, "I can see it in your eyes." Scary!

The people you love the most are generally the people you know the best. Dan and I share wonderful physical intimacy, but we often talk about the fact that in the last few years the most precious part of our relationship has become the deep intimacy we share as best friends and soul mates. That type of intimacy is precisely what God wants us to experience in our relationship with Him. God wants to be our eternal Soul Mate. He not only longs to hear my voice as I share the minute details of my life with Him, but He also wants me to hear His voice as He responds. Obviously, the Father is fully aware of every detail of my life before I share it with Him, but the sharing is for my good and creates a deeper bond between us. God wants me to know all about Him and long to be with Him. What an amazing possibility—to know the Living God as Lord, Savior, and Friend. That knowledge is the foundation of stress management.

God has a first name—"Yahweh" or "Jehovah"—a Hebrew word that means "I am." "LORD" should be translated "Jehovah," which means that Jehovah Almighty is His name. Jehovah is a personal name that reveals the very core of God's being, sufficiency, and holiness. God wants to be on a first name basis with us and wants us to come to Him just as we are, in our weakness and incompleteness. When we come before Him, sharing our deepest needs, with honesty and transparency, God then shares His last name, which is based on our current need in life.

God came to Moses and said, "I want you to be on a first name basis with me. My name is Jehovah" (see Genesis 3:14) and from that point on, whenever the people had a need they cried out in their insufficiency, saying, "God, You are the I Am. Come and meet me!" God would then come, meet them, and give them His last name. In Exodus the people cried, "God, we are out here in the desert with no food or water, literally starving to death! Jehovah, where are You?" Suddenly, quail are raining down from heaven and manna is found on the desert floor. God was Jehovah-Jireh, their Provider.

Later in Exodus, the people find themselves facing an immensely superior military force and cry out to God saying, "We can't do this! This army will wipe us out! Please help us!" God was then Jehovah-Nissi, which means "the Lord our Banner." In biblical times when tribes went to war, flags and banners were carried out in front. God assured His people that He would go before them and fight the battle for them.

In other passages, people came to God, overwhelmed and anxious. God says, "I am Jehovah-Shalom, your Peace." David came to Him in desperation and said, "God, I am in the wilderness and totally alone." God says, "I am Jehovah-Shammah. I am here."

God wants an intimate relationship with us. We can come to Him, calling Him by name, and He will meet the needs of our heart. Knowing God, and realizing that He knows us, is a powerful and strong foundation upon which we can build a peace-filled instead of a stress-controlled life.

God Loves Me

I believe much of our stress is the result of a constant and innate quest to love and be loved. The problems come when we look in the wrong places for love. When we know God, we know love. When we experience His unconditional love, we are then freed and empowered to love ourselves and others. I have personally discovered that it is just downright frustrating and completely impossible to live the Christian life when you are not a Christian. I tried.

For years I desperately struggled to be a Christian with only head knowledge of who God was and wanted to be in my life. The result was a pitifully shallow existence with stress and frustration as my constant companions.

I grew up in a Christian home, attending church every time the doors were open. I sang all of the right songs, spoke all of the right words and did all of the right things in front of all the right people. I fervently prayed that my works would validate my faith and desperately hoped that by following the rules, I would please the Ruler. It was not until middle school that the spiritual integrity of a dynamic youth pastor made me hunger and thirst for something more. I wanted to know God. I needed to experience the unconditional love of God.

During a special Saturday evening church service, I sat in my usual spot, clutching the back of the pew in front of me while wrestling with God over the condition of my soul and my eternal security. After all, even as a middle school student I was an active church member, a soloist and pianist for our worship services, and I even directed a children's choir. How embarrassing to walk down that aisle, admitting to everyone that I'd been living a lie. My mind argued that I knew all about God—and then the deeper truth of that argument hit me. Yes, I knew *about* Him, but I didn't *know* Him. His perfect love settles for nothing less than an intimate and loving relationship with His children. That night we met! I surrendered all that I knew about myself to all that I knew about Him. While the course of my life was changed forever, I quickly discovered that I still had to deal with stressful situations. The difference was that God's love preceded me and surrounded and sustained me as I lived each day. Knowing we are loved fosters contentment and peace in our hearts, and when our hearts are filled with peace, there is little room for stress.

God Chose Me

I can still remember the terror I felt each time my elementary teacher announced, "Today we are playing softball during recess." My stomach clenched in dread as I contemplated the tortuous hour stretching before me. I hated playing softball because I was a terrible athlete! Overweight, I huffed and puffed around the bases...if I ever got lucky enough to hit the elusive softball. I had no idea how to wear a softball glove, so the thought of actually trying to catch the ball was terrifying. I was always assigned to the outfield, where few balls came and where I had the least chance of doing any damage. The most horrible part of the whole experience was the dreaded team selection process. It was always the same. Two captains were chosen, usually Sarah and Tim because they were slender, attractive, and popular—everything I wasn't. Sarah and Tim would step to the pitcher's mound and begin the process of choosing their teams. I can still remember trying to look as if I didn't care that everyone around me was moving to one side or the other while I waited, praying that I would hear my name called by somebody...anybody. I was usually one of three or four children left standing, staring at the preferred ones already taking their positions on the field. Sarah usually took pity on me and picked me before Jeff and Alicia. At least I wasn't the last one chosen.

We tend to find our identity and worth in the fact that we are chosen by someone. Every shepherd chose his sheep—one by one—with great deliberation, thought, and care. A choice implies ownership, pursuit, and a deliberate action on the part of the one doing the choosing.

I have spent a great deal of my time and energy in an ongoing attempt to validate my identity. Much of the pain, frustration, and stress I've experienced could have been avoided by simply remembering whose I am—a chosen child, a daughter of the King, and an indispensable part of God's heart. That's right! I am indispensable to no one but God. No one can take my place in my Father's heart.

The knowledge that I'm chosen frees me to serve Him wholeheartedly and boldly without bowing to unrealistic expectations imposed by others and my own fragile heart. The knowledge that He created me allows me to embrace the gifts He has given me and encourages me to strain every choice, every decision, through the filter of His perfect plan for my life. Knowing whose I am draws my attention away from both the critics and the cheerleaders in life and fixes my gaze on the *only* one I have to please...God.

Knowing whose we are settles our souls and directs our steps toward the path God intended when He shaped us. You and I were created as a living, fleshed-out interpretation of God's love. We can celebrate the precious truth of Psalm 139:14-16:

I praise you because you made me in an amazing and wonderful way. What you have done is wonderful. I know this very well. You saw my bones being formed as I took shape in my mother's body. When I was put together there, you saw my body as it was formed. All the days planned for me were written in your book before I was one day old (NCV).

Just think of it! God Himself supervised our formation. We were created in love—for love—with a specific and holy purpose in mind. We can rejoice with the psalmist who wrote, "Know that the Lord is God. He made us, and we belong to him; we are his people, the sheep he tends" (Psalm 100:3 NCV).

God is an up close and personal God. He met Nicodemus at night (John 3:1-21), He met the sinful woman at the well of Samaria (John 4:1-42), He met the crippled man at the pool of Bethesda (John 5:1-9), and He touched a blind man, giving him sight (John 9:1-7). As he walked through Jericho, Jesus saw a little man perched in a tree and called to him, "Zacchaeus, come down immediately. I must stay at your house today" (Luke 19:1-6). He met Matthew at the tax collector's booth and told him, "Follow me" (Matthew 9:9). We come to Jesus alone. There are no group rates when it comes to knowing God. It's always one-on-one and personal. What you believe about God in the silence and stillness of your own heart is what makes the difference in your life journey. The heart is where all spiritual transactions are made and the transformation process begins. "He calls his own sheep by name" (John 10:3).

Stress is a deadly disease that can wreak havoc in our lives. The frightening reality is that stress seems to run rampant and in epidemic proportions through relationships, jobs, homes, and every part of who we are. It doesn't have to be that way. In fact, a stress-riddled existence has never been and will never be part of God's plan for His children. On the other hand, Satan's plan for us definitely includes stress because he knows that stress is a powerful tool through which he can work. Stress is his invitation to set up shop in our lives.

Remember, stress management begins with a personal relationship with God. Without Him, we are in eternal trouble. A little girl ended her bedtime prayer with "Dear God, I need You to please take care of Mommy, take care of Daddy, take care of my sister and my brother, and please, please God, take care of Yourself, because if You don't we're all sunk. Amen."

I couldn't have said it better myself.

Stress-Busters

Meet **Ellen Briggs,** Food Consultant, and **Sally Byrd, N.D.**, authors of *Are Your Kids Running on Empty?* and *Mom, I'm Hungry. What's for Dinner* (Many Hands Publishing, 2004).

From Ellen and Sally

The Lord created every part of you! Your brain and muscles are 75 percent water. Your lungs are 90 percent. Skin, blood, kidneys, and digestive juices are between 80 and 86 percent water. The toxin removal organ, the liver, is 69 percent water. Only your bones contain a small amount of water, between 22 and 25 percent. In order to nourish the trillions of cells comprising all the systems in your body, you must drink a lot of water.

Here's an easy-to-remember formula: Drink half your body weight in ounces. For example, if you weigh 144 pounds, you should drink 72 ounces or 9 cups of water a day. When you are losing water due to physical activity or heat, drink more. If your mouth feels dry, you are about 3 percent dehydrated. When you lose 5 percent of your water supply, your mental and physical performance declines by about 30 percent, is malnourished, and stressed. Consequently, internal systems break down. You were created to be God's efficient, well-functioning servant. You are the steward of the temple He gave you.

○ ○ ○

- Maintain a healthy diet. Even doing so 80 percent of the time will produce great benefits.

- Laugh…a lot!

- Do something every day for the "child" in you.

- Have a good cry. Tears resulting from sadness, anger, fear, or joy vary chemically from those caused by chopping onions and are one of nature's methods of removing chemicals built up by stress in the body.

- Pray about everything. If it's important to you, it's important to God.

- Record favorite Scriptures on 3x5 cards and keep them on hand to read throughout the day.

- Separate baseless worries from genuine concerns. If a situation is a concern, find out what God wants you to do about it and then do it. If you can't do anything about a situation, let it go.

- Create a personal CD of songs guaranteed to make you smile. Listen to it whenever you need a lift. For the ultimate stress-buster, pop it in and dance your heart out!

- Carry a pocket-size Bible with you to read in waiting rooms.

S tock up on anything chocolate—ice cream, candy, or cookies. Even chocolate covered raisins will do.

T uck yourself in bed, curl up under the covers in a fetal position, and stay there as long as possible…preferably with the above chocolate cache.

R etreat to your collection of DVDs.

E ntertain yourself with a cheesy mystery novel.

S tay in your pajamas all day while watching the Home and Garden Network, the Travel Channel, or the Food Channel.

S eek guidance from a trusted friend who will give you godly counsel to break free of the stress bondage.

2

Recognize Your Source

I shall not want.
PSALM 23:1 NKJV

Jehovah-Jireh: *The Lord Will Provide*

~ The Shepherd and His Sheep ~

Shepherds live with their sheep, finding places for them to feed and drink, and providing shelter from storms and protection from the heat. Sheep must eat the right amount of the right kinds of grass at the right times or they will die. If the sheep eat too little one day and too much the next day, some of the bacteria which live in the stomach of the sheep will reproduce at abnormal levels, creating toxins that cause sudden death. This problem was even more complex for the shepherds of the Bible. The type of shepherding referred to in the Bible is not the farming of fenced pasture lands but nomadic grazing. The shepherd must carefully plan the path and lead the way so that the sheep have neither too little nor too much grazing and are able to get to the water hole on time.

Pastures were often lost to extreme heat, which meant the shepherd had to scour the countryside in search of green grass. Several flocks of sheep are gathered together at night in a sheltered place so shepherds can share the watches of the night and protect the sheep from wild animals and thieves. Good shepherds are always willing to risk their lives to save their flocks from any harm, any enemy, and even from themselves.

The needs of sheep, compared to the needs of other animals, tend to be greater because of their instinct to be afraid and, when faced with a fearful situation, to run. Without a shepherd to care for the sheep, they wouldn't last long. Sheep are dumb. They can never be left alone and often stray, requiring the shepherd to find and rescue them. A shepherd never *pushes* his sheep but rather *leads* them, going before them and making sure they are not walking into danger.

○ ○ ○

I love the well-known story of the Sunday school teacher who asked the children in her class to quote their favorite Bible verse. She often had to coax them into standing and sharing, but one Sunday, when she asked if anyone had a verse to share, a little boy's hand immediately shot into the air! The teacher was so pleased. "Johnny, will you share your favorite verse with us?" The little boy stood tall as he spoke. "The Lord is my shepherd. He's all I want." The teacher thought about correcting him but then realized that while he may have quoted the verse wrong, the little boy certainly had grasped its true meaning.

Hmm...I don't know about you, but there are a lot of things I want—material things, good health, success in ministry, replenishing relationships, to be loved and appreciated—the list is endless. However, I invariably find myself in spiritual chaos when God isn't *all* I want. In this psalm "want" means "lack" and refers to the inheritance that is ours as children of the King. That's right! The moment you surrendered your heart and life to God through a personal relationship with Jesus Christ, you were granted an eternal inheritance.

I, along with almost every other female in the world, have wondered what the life of an heiress would be like. Visions of designer clothes, rich furs, sparkling jewels, luxury cars, great wealth, and personal servants have danced across my dreams from time to time. The reality, however, is that I already am an heiress but often fail to recognize and walk in the incredible wealth that is mine. My Father is rich! He owns it all! What a promise God gives—to know we will never lack a single thing we need.

We tend to think that "I shall not want" refers to material possessions alone. In fact, it's probably easier for many of us to address the issues of materialism rather than facing those darker longings of our very human and self-serving hearts. While materialistic hunger is a constant and troublesome craving, even greater longings nudge us toward danger. Emotional needs that are met in wrong ways can easily destroy a marriage. The desire for success can plunge us into a deep, dark pit of burnout and exhaustion, derailing the plan of God in our lives. Pride flourishes, masked in our carefully constructed lies of humility and compliance. Outwardly, we feign a submissive heart while inwardly ego reigns, veiled in a false obedience and artificial commitment. Just as a loving father meets the needs of his children, God meets our needs.

Every morning the little old lady stepped onto her front porch, raised her arms to the sky, and shouted, "Praise the Lord!" One day an atheist moved into the house next door and soon became irritated with the little old lady's morning ritual. Every morning he would step onto his front porch after her and yell, "There is no God!" Time passed with the two of them carrying on this way until one winter morning when the little old lady stepped onto her front porch and shouted, "Praise the Lord! I have no food and I am starving. Please provide for me, Lord!" When she stepped onto her porch the next day, there sat two huge bags of groceries. "Praise the Lord!" she cried out. "God has provided!" The atheist neighbor jumped out of the hedges and shouted, "Ha! See? There is no God. I provided those groceries!" The little old lady once again threw her arms into the air and shouted, "Praise the Lord! He has provided me with groceries and made the devil pay for them!" God may not always provide in the way we might have chosen, but He always provides. He is our source.

I really believe that a large part of our stress is the result of misplaced expectations, requiring the people and circumstances in our lives to meet needs only God can meet. Most people who know me well would tell you that I'm a very strong woman. It took a complete physical, emotional, and spiritual breakdown for me to realize that I was only as strong as my human personality and abilities would allow me to be. I was, in short, looking in all the wrong places for the deepest needs of my heart to be met. When everything was stripped away by a two-year battle with clinical depression, I was left with nothing but broken dreams and unanswered questions. There, in that dark pit, surrounded by the surprisingly meager remains of a shattered life, I discovered that God is enough. What happens when we live as if He is not enough and He is not all we want? Greed happens! And stress always tags along behind greed.

After a Saturday night worship service, Dan was in his usual spot, down front, talking with those who had made a decision for Christ that night and meeting first-time visitors to Flamingo Road Church. As I looked over the crowd gathered around my husband, I noticed Kelly, the five-year-old daughter of our worship leader, sitting on the edge of the platform, patiently waiting for Dan. After several minutes, Kelly was obviously tired of waiting. She spotted me sitting in the first row and evidently decided I would have to do.

Jumping off of the stage, she headed straight for me, grinning and pointing to her mouth. "Mimi, guess what? I lost a tooth!" Carefully examining the illustrious gap, I exclaimed, "That's great, sweetie! The tooth fairy will definitely come tonight!" A mischievous grin spread across her face as she responded, "Oh, he already came last night and brought me five dollars. So my mom took me to the mall today and I bought lots of stuff!" Tooth loss has definitely evolved over the years. "That's wonderful, Kelly," I exclaimed, giving her a big hug. However, she didn't hug me back and, in fact, seemed disappointed. I was confused and obviously missing some important point. Kelly's next words explained it all. "Yes, but Pastor Dan always gives me money when I lose a tooth!" Ah, the truth comes out. Reaching for my purse, I pulled out a dollar and pressed it into Kelly's outstretched hand. With longing in her eyes, she gazed at the money and softly said, "I wish this dollar was really five dollars so I could go back to the mall and buy more stuff." And there you have the very heart of man. We were born greedy and got worse—just like Sapphira, a woman consumed by greed.

Sapphira was a part of the growing Christian community during the first century, an exciting time to be alive. Peter had preached a powerful message at Pentecost, which turned into a major spiritual awakening as 3000 people came to Christ (Acts 2:14-41). This early group of believers loved God and each other. In fact, they met together daily to worship God and even sold their houses and lands, using the money for the good of everyone. Among this group was a married couple named Ananias and Sapphira, believers who wanted to get in on the recognition of giving. The couple sold a piece of property so the church leaders could use the proceeds to help the needy, but once they had the money in hand, they decided to deposit part of the proceeds from the sale in a rainy day account...just in case! Now, there's nothing wrong with that decision, right? However, they then decided to lie and say they were really giving all of the money to God, just as they had originally planned. Greed has power in our lives only when we grant it power, a grave mistake on the part of Ananias and Sapphira. Theirs is not only an ugly story, but uncomfortably familiar as well:

> A man named Ananias and his wife Sapphira sold some land. He kept back part of the money for himself; his wife knew about this and agreed to it. But he brought the rest of the money and gave it to the apostles. Peter said, "Ananias, why

did you let Satan rule your thoughts to lie to the Holy Spirit and to keep for yourself part of the money you received for the land? Before you sold the land, it belonged to you. And even after you sold it, you could have used the money any way you wanted. Why did you think of doing this? You lied to God, not to us!" When Ananias heard this, he fell down and died. Some young men came in, wrapped up his body, carried it out, and buried it. And everyone who heard about this was filled with fear. About three hours later his wife came in, but she did not know what had happened. Peter said to her, "Tell me, was the money you got for your field this much?" Sapphira answered, "Yes. That was the price." Peter said to her, "Why did you and your husband agree to test the Spirit of the Lord? Look! The men who buried your husband are at the door, and they will carry you out." At that moment, Sapphira fell down by his feet and died. When the young men came in and saw that she was dead they carried her out and buried her beside her husband" (Acts 5:1-10 NCV).

Greed is serious business in God's eyes. Greed reeks of idolatry and ulterior motives. Greed lies easily and fervently urges an already disobedient heart toward sin, the bedrock of stress. In order to manage stress, conquer greed, control our wants, and honor God while depending upon Him as our source for every need, we must make several choices.

Choice One: Avoid Greedy People

Do not envy wicked men, do not desire their company (Proverbs 24:1).

Greed is contagious. If we spend time with people who are prone to jealousy and greed, it will be easier for us to become jealous and greedy as well.

When anyone in our house gets sick, they know what is coming.

A war! The battle against illness begins, Mom against the germs! I head to the store to stock up on basic combat supplies. The list is usually the same: juice, soup, crackers, yogurt, throat lozenges, tissues, cold medicine, and, last, but certainly not least, several cans of Lysol. I then implement my battle plan. The "sickie" is confined to their quarters and is allotted one bathroom, one sofa, and one bedroom for the duration of their illness. The ailing one is not to enter any other area of the barracks without my permission. I then go room to room, spraying every surface they may have touched or even thought about touching. While the patient is allowed to continue breathing, I tend to follow the feeble one around, spraying the air that borders each breath. The sanitizing procedure continues until the patient is completely well. I know. I am obnoxious, but I am also successful more times than not in my quest to prevent the spread of germs and illness. I don't want to catch their disease and feel it's my responsibility to quarantine the sick ones in order to halt the progression of their sickness.

Greed is a noxious disease, one that demands immediate and fierce spiritual quarantine. We must be careful that we don't catch the spirit of greed and jealousy. Steer clear of those people who are prone to this deadly disease.

Choice Two: Examine Every Heart Motive

> There were no needy persons among them. For from time to time those who owned lands or houses sold them, brought the money from the sales and put it at the apostles' feet, and it was distributed to anyone as he had need (Acts 4:34-35).

The greed of Ananias and Sapphira emerged from the wrong heart motive of pride and developed into a full-blown case of greed. The believers were selling their possessions, pooling their resources, and helping those in need. One of the believers, Barnabas, had sold a piece of land he owned and had given all of the proceeds from that sale to the church (Acts 4:36). Everyone was talking about him and the good example he had set. Ananias and Sapphira wanted that same recognition. Their gift was acceptable, but their motive wasn't. God is always more interested in our motive for giving than in the gift itself, and He is neither interested nor pleased by a gift given from a prideful or greedy heart. Greed is not only ugly and powerful; it has friends who are even worse!

> For from within, out of men's hearts, come evil thoughts, sexual immorality, theft, murder, adultery, greed, malice, deceit, lewdness, envy, slander, arrogance and folly (Mark 7:21-22).

Greed is an inside job, invading our thoughts and then taking up residence in a discontented heart as it opens the door for other stress-induced and deadly sins. The warning of Proverbs 4:23 is clear, "Above all else, guard your heart, for it affects everything you do" (NLT). Ananias and Sapphira loved money and craved the approval of man. That love of money did them in. Their ungodly hunger for man's approval destroyed them. Greed and honesty cannot exist in the same heart, and God wants us to give with an honest heart. "I know, my God, that you test people's hearts. You are happy when people do what is right. I was happy to give all these things, and I gave with an honest heart" (1 Chronicles 29:17 NCV). In this verse "honest" means "with integrity." To give with integrity means to give the right thing at the right time, to the right person for the right reason, a reason that always originates in love—God's love—a love that has been given to us in order for us to give it away in His name. The circle of giving is a circle of love, and it all started with God when He gave His one and only Son, Jesus Christ.

> God loved the world so much that he gave his one and only Son (John 3:16 NCV).

We are loved, so we give love. And because we give love, we will receive love. Matthew 7:2 says, "The amount you give to others will be given to you" (NCV). Luke 6:38 offers a clear picture of God's giving plan: "Give, and you will receive. You will be given much.

Pressed down, shaken together, and running over, it will spill into your lap. The way you give to others is the way God will give to you" (NCV). What and how we give determines what and how much we receive. We simply cannot out-give God! I have heard it said that the Lord loves a cheerful giver but will even accept an offering from a grouch. I have also heard it said that plenty of people are willing to give God credit but few are willing to give Him cash. The truth is that the Father looks past the gift and examines the heart behind the gift because the motive of the heart determines the acceptability of the gift.

A little boy went to see Santa at the neighborhood mall. When Santa asked him what he wanted for Christmas, the little boy pulled out his list and began to read: "I want two toy trucks, two teddy bears, two remote control cars, and two video games." Santa remarked, "That certainly is a tall order. Do you mind telling me why you want two of everything?" The little boy quickly answered, "So I can share!" That's the right idea.

> Tell those who are rich in this world not to be proud and not to trust in their money, which will soon be gone. But their trust should be in the living God, who richly gives us all we need for our enjoyment. Tell them to use their money to do good. They should be rich in good works and should give generously to those in need, always being ready to share with others whatever God has given them. By doing this they will be storing up their treasure as a good foundation for the future so that they may take hold of real life (1 Timothy 6:17-19 NLT).

I am afraid we are often like Ananias and Sapphira in that our heart motives are suspect when it comes to giving. Our pride is at stake, so we give to impress others. We give out of fear and guilt, hoping to buy God's forgiveness for sin. People are watching, so we give in order to gain their approval. Giving is a powerful and effective deterrent to greed when we give for no other reason than the joy of giving.

The true story is told of a self-made millionaire who was born and raised in the ghettos of New York City. He worked hard and achieved much. Anyone who knew this man would testify to the fact that he was generous—to a fault, some would say. One year, the man was disturbed by an attitude of selfishness and greed that seemed to pervade the Christmas holiday season and everyone around him. Not one to condemn, the millionaire decided that since he'd been given so much, it was up to him to do his part in combating greed and came up with an unusual plan. Wearing a disguise, this man stuffed his pockets with $100 bills and set out for a walk on the streets of New York City. When he saw someone in need, he whipped out one of the bills, pressed it into that person's hands, and, with a "Merry Christmas," made his way down the street. "It was the most wonderful part of my holiday season," the man reported, and he has been doing it every since.

The apostle Paul writes, "Each one should give as you have decided in your heart to give. You should not be sad when you give, and you should not give because you feel forced to give. God loves the person who gives happily" (2 Corinthians 9:7 NCV). Giving with joy is kingdom giving! When we practice kingdom giving, we are making eternal deposits and "taking hold of real life" (1 Timothy 6:19 NLT) here on earth. If, however, our motive is wrong, our gift will be wrong and will not count in the kingdom of God. Before you give, ask yourself, "What's in it for me?" If the answer is "nothing," then go ahead and give the gift. Choosing to examine heart motives will guard our hearts against greed and celebrate the commitment that "He is all I want."

Greed can be very stressful in that it's never satisfied and never at rest. There is always something more to be gained and someone else to outdo. Sheep are dumb enough to eat until they are sick. They simply don't know when to stop. A heart that is filled with greed behaves the same way.

Cantaloupe is definitely one of my favorite fruits. Last summer, on a particularly hot day, a lunch of cantaloupe sounded luscious…and it was. Afterward, I had a long list of errands to run and was gone several hours. When I walked back in the front door, a foul stench nearly knocked me down. A dead animal was my first thought. A plumbing problem was my next. I began a room-to-room search that ended abruptly at the kitchen sink. Opening the cabinet underneath, I nearly gagged at the stench that slapped me in the face, making my eyes water. I instantly remembered that I had thrown the cantaloupe peels in the garbage before running errands and forgotten to take them to the outside garbage can as I usually did. The house reeked and the delicious cantaloupe was forgotten as I threw the peels away, lit every candle I could find, and opened every window in an effort to eliminate the odor of rotting fruit.

Greed acts the same way. It is the gangrene of the soul. If not quickly dealt with, greed will contaminate every emotion and create a foul stench in every part of life. "So get rid of all malicious behavior and deceit. Don't just pretend to be good! Be done with hypocrisy and jealousy and backstabbing" (1 Peter 2:1 NLT). Greed must be treated just like garbage. Deliberately throw it away. Remove it from your life immediately. In 2 Corinthians 7:1 we find the apostle Paul's strong warning to "purify ourselves from everything that contaminates body and spirit, perfecting holiness out of reverence for God." When the first hint of greed and jealousy comes, reject it. Get rid of it. Take it to the garbage. Choose against it. Fight it with Scripture and bombard it with prayer. Nail it to the cross and count it dead. "I have been crucified with Christ and I no longer live, but Christ lives in me. The life I live in the body, I live by faith in the Son of God, who loved me and gave himself for me" (Galatians 2:20). Every wrong motive must be nailed to the cross and considered dead. "Consider" is an accounting term that means to "reckon" or to "calculate." While we will never be totally free from wrong motives this side of heaven, we can and must "reckon" those very human and very wrong motives to be dead and through God's power, allocate them no place in our heart.

Choice Three: Hold Stuff Loosely

> A man named Ananias and his wife Sapphira sold some land. He kept back part of the money for himself; his wife knew about this and agreed to it (Acts 5:1-2 NCV).

> When they refused to acknowledge God, he abandoned them to their evil minds and let them do things that should never be done. Their lives became full of every kind of wickedness, sin, greed, hate, envy, murder, fighting, deception, malicious behavior, and gossip (Romans 1:28-29 NLT).

Greed and jealousy are offsprings of idolatry. The reality is that we want whatever we put first in life. I've discovered that the more I have to live for, the less I need to live on. Luke writes, "Jesus said to them, 'Be careful and guard against all kinds of greed. Life is not measured by how much one owns'" (Luke 12:15 NCV).

Corrie Ten Boom was a godly woman who endured great persecution from the Nazis in a World War II concentration camp. Years later she stated in an interview that she had learned to hold everything loosely in her hands. When asked why, Miss Ten Boom explained that she had discovered that when she grasped things tightly, it hurt more when the Lord would have to pry her fingers loose.

We live in a stuff-driven world where it doesn't seem to matter what we have; it's never enough. We are told the more things we have, the more successful we are. We not only covet possessions, we crave other people's talents, abilities, circumstances, relationships...we want it all. We are driven to have the best and to be the best, unable to relax and appreciate where we are and what we have. No wonder we are stressed out! Hebrews 13:5 is powerfully clear in its warning: "Keep your lives free from the love of money, and be satisfied with what you have. God has said, 'I will never leave you; I will never forget you'" (NCV). Now that is a fortune!

How important are your possessions? How do you view them? Howard Hendricks, a great Bible teacher, was having dinner with a very wealthy and prestigious man. Hendricks was amazed at the humility of his host, knowing the man's impressive credentials and the massive wealth he possessed. At the end of the evening, Hendricks asked his friend, "How did you grow up in such wealth and not be consumed by materialism?" With a smile, the man responded, "My parents taught me that everything in our home was either an idol or a tool. The choice was up to me."

Everything in life is either an idol we choose to worship or a tool we choose to use for either good or bad. The choice really is ours to make. We need to hold our stuff loosely while investing financial resources in the things that are eternal. To stay away from idols and avoid greed, we need to change our focus from what we want to what we have and choose to be satisfied with whatever that is.

If we want to escape the stress trap, we must choose to put things in their proper place and refuse to attach importance to them. I believe that attaching importance to things is sin and will lead to more sin. The monster of greed is fed by fear, a sin that was certainly present in the lives of Ananias and Sapphira. They were afraid of giving it all. They were afraid of not having enough. They were afraid to sacrifice. They were afraid of not gaining approval and not having enough resources for the future. How important are your possessions? How do you view the things you own?

One way we can guard against greed and control our wants is to view our possessions as resources loaned to us by God for us to disperse instead of treating them as earned rewards or deserved pleasures. "Each one should use whatever gift he has received to serve others" (I Peter 4:10). Every spiritual gift, every financial resource, and every possession has been given to us by God as a way to serve others. Greed steps in the minute we begin to view those gifts and resources as our own, clutching them tightly in our hands and in our hearts. Fear then leads us to worry about losing what is not really ours to begin with and, left unchecked, greed can lead to dishonesty. Peter asked, "Ananias, why did you let Satan rule your thought to lie to the Holy Spirit and to keep for yourself part of the money you received for the land?" (Acts 5:3 NCV). In this verse, "rule" means "to control." Greed and exaggerated wants controlled both Ananias and Sapphira to the point that they were consumed by a fear which naturally led to dishonesty and lies. The sad part is that their lie was an unnecessary lie. No one was forcing them to sell the land in the first place, but greed offered the invitation to sin and they accepted. Furthermore, they didn't have to give all of the money but could have given part and kept part of the proceeds from the sale. "Before you sold the land, it belonged to you. And even after you sold it, you could have used the money any way you wanted. Why did you think of doing this? You lied to God, not to us!" (Acts 5:4 NCV). The greed for approval and financial security became a seed of dishonesty in the hearts of Ananias and Sapphira, eventually grew into deceit, and drove them to hypocrisy.

The story is told of the world's stingiest man who went shopping for a friend's gift. Everything was too expensive, except for a $50 vase that was on sale for $2.00 because the handle had been broken off. The stingy man bought it and had the salesman ship it so his friend would think he had paid the full $50 for it and that it had been broken in shipment. A week later the penny-pinching man received a thank-you note from his friend. "Thank you for the lovely vase," the note read. "It was so nice of you to wrap each piece separately." The reality is that who we are should never be measured in terms of what we have or don't have. Instead, our lives are measured by who and what we are. Ananias and Sapphira thought they were lying to Peter and the other believers, when their dishonesty was actually directed toward God.

The lure of material wealth is often stronger than the human will and always positions itself between us and God. The result will always be stress. Someday, I think we will discover that heaven's door is covered with silver and gold, shutting out those who worship riches.

I love the story of a wealthy man who prayed, asking for permission to take his earthly wealth with him when he died and went to heaven. An angel appeared to the man and said, "We heard your prayer, but I'm sorry. You simply cannot take it with you." The man pleaded so passionately that the angel said, "Let me see what I can do." When the angel returned, he reported, "Good news! God has made an exception for you. You may bring one suitcase with you when it's your time to go." Delighted, the man packed his one suitcase and went on with life. Several years later, he died and appeared at the Pearly Gates, where he was met by Saint Peter, who took one look at the suitcase and said, "I am sorry, sir, but you cannot bring that in with you." The man protested, "But I received special permission." Just then, the angel appeared and said, "Peter, it's true. He has special permission to bring one suitcase in with him." Curious, Peter said, "Do you mind showing me what's in the bag that is so important to you?" With a smile, the man replied, "Not at all" and proceeded to open the suitcase to reveal stacks of gold bricks. Peter's shock was apparent as he blurted out, "Pavement? You brought pavement with you?"

Stress thrives on greed that urges us on, in a never-ending and futile quest to accumulate "pavement" *here* that is totally worthless *there*. Wealth is all a matter of perspective. We need to understand that our Father wants us to have wealth. We just have to be careful that we don't settle for earthly money and possessions instead of eternal treasures.

Choice Four: Trust God to Provide

Ananias and Sapphira had seen God do great things and had heard Peter preach about the death, burial, and resurrection of Jesus. Thousands of lives had been changed before their very eyes. Ananias and Sapphira professed to believe in God and to be followers of Christ, but they didn't trust God enough to give Him all their money. The reality is that they did not trust God to provide for them and that lack of trust led to their deaths.

We need to understand and dwell in the truth that God is our source. Psalm 23:1 says, "I shall not want" (NKJV). In this verse, "want" means "lack." God will see to it that His children lack nothing. He will provide. God will take care of us, supplying every need, and not just material needs. He meets every emotional need, every physical need, and every mental need. Our mate is not our source. Our job is not our source. Our children are not our source. God is our source.

Christmas is my favorite time of the year. One of my favorite family traditions is the buying of our Christmas tree. It must be purchased on the day after Thanksgiving and it must be purchased from the nice man who runs a tree lot just down the street from our house because he has the best Fraser Firs in town. The whole process is steeped in Southerland tradition.

We all pile into "Old Blue," my husband's well-worn truck, and head for the tree lot. When we arrive, my husband and our children fan out in search of "the tree." Yes, I believe there is one particular tree just waiting for us to claim it. Over the years many people have tried to change that opinion, but I'm standing firm. As tradition demands, Dan immediately begins muttering, "Bah, humbug" under his breath but just loud enough for us all to hear him. That is the cue for our daughter, Danna, to begin rolling her eyes and correcting her Scrooge father. Our son, Jered, ignores them both and carries out his steady search in quiet contemplation. He usually spots "the tree" first. "Found it!" he will shout, which is another verbal tree-finding tradition. We all gather to inspect Jered's find, immediately dismiss it as unworthy, and spread out once again in search of our tree.

The owners of the tree lot now sense the nonnegotiable Southerland step-by-step process and stand back, waiting for the curtain to fall on the tree drama, content in the knowledge that we will eventually buy a tree from them. I consider and dismiss almost every tree on the lot before going back to the first tree Jered picked. Afraid of losing his tree to another customer, Jered faithfully stands guard until we all come to our senses and realize that he, once again, has found the perfect tree. After what we consider a respectable search time, we once again gather at Jered's tree to evaluate each side to make sure it will display well and, finally, examine the top of the tree to make sure our angel treetopper will be comfortable there.

The moment of truth arrives when Dan, Danna, and Jered all look at me and ask, "Well, what do you think, Mom? Is this the one?" Savoring the moment, I take my time, circling the tree in quiet appraisal. My husband and children know that, at this point, their only job is to remain silent. Finally I turn to them and say, "Let's get it!" I am almost certain I hear applause at this moment, from my family, from other customers, and certainly from the tree man. My husband writes the check as Jered loads the tree in Old Blue and we head home, where the Christmas tree stand is ready and waiting. Jered, a husky football player, unloads the tree, cuts off an inch of the trunk, places it in the stand, and transports the tree to its new home for the holidays.

The smell is delicious. The needles are green and fresh...for about a month, and then, every year, the same sad process begins. Although I faithfully water the tree, the needles grow more brittle with each day that passes, the smell is less powerful, and eventually, the limbs begin to wither, dry out, and turn brown. Why? The tree has been separated from its source. The same is true in our lives.

I am convinced that a great deal of our stress is born in wrong priorities and fed by inadequate sources. As a result, we are never quite satisfied as we desperately try to squeeze life out of lifeless things. God is our sole provider. Yet I often find myself afraid to let go, refusing to give back to God what really belongs to Him in the first place. "The LORD is my shepherd; I shall not want." When it comes to the resources we need for life, this promise from the Twenty-third Psalm is staggeringly important to remember.

A famous actor was once the guest of honor at a social gathering where he was asked to recite favorite excerpts from various literary works. An old preacher who happened to be there asked the actor to recite the Twenty-third Psalm. The actor agreed on the condition that the preacher would also recite it. The actor's recitation was beautifully intoned with great dramatic emphasis, for which he received lengthy applause. The preacher's voice was rough and broken from many years of preaching, and his diction was anything but polished, but when he finished, there was not a dry eye in the room. When someone asked the actor what made the difference, he simply replied, "I know the psalm, but he knows the Shepherd."

> Who is wise and understanding among you? Let him show it by his good life, by deeds done in the humility that comes from wisdom. But if you harbor bitter envy and selfish ambition in your hearts, do not boast about it or deny the truth. Such "wisdom" does not come down from heaven but is earthly, unspiritual, of the devil. For where you have envy and selfish ambition, there you find disorder and every evil practice (James 3:13-16).

James asks who is wise and understanding. In this passage, "wise" describes someone with moral insight, someone with skill in the practical issues of life. "Understanding" describes an "intellectual perception." James then calls for a spiritual "show and tell." "Let him show it by his good life, by deeds done in the humility that comes from wisdom" (verse 13). James is sending us a strong message. Wisdom and understanding are not measured by degrees, but by deeds. In other words, it's not how much we know that counts, but rather how much we are living that matters. We can talk a great spiritual game, but if we have a greedy heart, if we harbor jealousy or allow envy to creep into our lives, influencing us in any way, we have no wisdom and are living a lie. So the question then becomes, what steps can we take to avoid jealousy and the stress it brings?

James warns against "bitter envy," which means "a nasty jealousy," while "selfish ambition" indicates "a contentious selfishness or a hostile ego." "Selfish ambition" can also be translated as a "party spirit" and was used by the Greeks to describe a dishonest politician who works the crowd, using every opportunity and every possible method to garner attention in an attempt to win votes. James is undoubtedly painting an ugly picture of jealousy at work. A jealous person tears others down in order to build himself up.

I once read about a fisherman who loved to catch crabs. After many years of crabbing, he finally learned he never needed a top for his crab basket because if one of the crabs starts to climb up the sides of the basket, the other crabs will reach up and pull it back down. What a perfect picture of jealousy. And what a perfect picture of our world, a place where we tear each other down in order to make ourselves look good. Sadly, Paul makes the point that jealousy is not only rampant in the world, but among believers as well. "You are still controlled by your own sinful desires. You are jealous of one another and quarrel with each other. Doesn't that prove you are controlled by your own desires? You are acting like people who don't belong to the Lord" (1 Corinthians 3:3 NLT). People of the world are driven by ego. People of the world want what everyone else has, are suspicious of most, trust no one, and resent the success of everyone. People of the world are taught by greed and jealousy to take care of self above all others, an attitude riddled with stress.

John and Dave were hiking when they spotted a mountain lion staring at them. John froze in his tracks while Dave sat down on a log, tore off his hiking boots, pulled a pair of running shoes from his backpack, and quickly put them on. John looked at him in amazement. "What are you thinking? You can't outrun a mountain lion!" Dave shrugged and simply said, "I don't have to. I just have to outrun you." We live in a "me first" world where greed and jealousy spring from hearts of insecurity and bubble out in a bevy of self-centered actions, arrogant words, and selfish attitudes. We need to remember Paul's warning that greed is deadly. The only cure for greed is to train our heart attitudes to reflect the truth that God alone is our provider. He is all we need.

Have you noticed that it is always more fun to pay the bills when you actually *have* money to pay them instead of holding what my husband calls "The Monthly Draw"? The Southerland Monthly Draw is held when there are more bills than money. The rules are quite simple. All of the bills are placed in a stack. Dan then rifles through the stack, drawing out one of the bills to pay. This process continues until there is no more money.

When I walked into the study one morning, I could tell by the look on Dan's face that the "draw" was not going well. Finances had been extremely tight. Dan and I had prayed our way through that month, knowing that the next few months would hold more of the same. I debated whether I should stick around to offer encouragement or run for the hills. I decided to stay. "Honey, can I help?" Dan looked up at me with a weak grin and said, "Not unless you have nine hundred dollars." Oh, boy! It was worse than I thought. Seeing the look on my face, my sweet husband quickly added, "Don't worry, honey. God always comes through." Now I must admit that at that precise moment, I would have preferred a tangible sample of God's provision. You know—something along the lines of a money tree in the backyard or an oil well in the front. I went to my desk, hoping to find a forgotten check from a speaking event or book sale. I came up empty. An examination of my check register was even more depressing. Did we really need two children? Maybe we should sell one. As I racked my brain for some way to "provide," I realized that I was stepping dangerously close to Sapphira Territory. "Lord, I want to trust You as my Provider, but right now we really need nine hundred dollars." How is that for a prayer of faith?

Dan did all he could do with the stack of bills and went next door to visit our neighbor while I stayed home, plotting and scheming ways to come up with the needed funds. In fact, I spent the rest of the day in what my mother called "a tizzy" because as far as I could see, there was no plot and there was no scheme remotely looming in the Southerland picture that could produce the required amount of money. And that was the problem. I was only looking as far as I could see.

Finally, I left the need at His feet and went on with what was left of my day. As I prepared dinner, I remembered that I had forgotten to check the mail and headed outside. There it was, God's perfect provision just sitting in our mailbox, waiting for me to come—an unexpected check for $949.64. I became aware of the need that morning. The check was mailed days before. God met the need before the need was evident. He always does!

Just as the shepherd meets every need of his sheep, God meets our every need. Just as the sheep totally depend upon their shepherd's care, we would be wise to depend totally upon God. He is our Provider. He is our Source, and in light of that reality, stress flees, leaving only peace.

My Psalm 23

The Lord is my Shepherd
You are my Identity

I shall not want
You are my Provision

He makes me to lie down in green pastures
You are my Rest

He leads me beside the still waters
You are my Replenishment

He restores my soul
You are my Healing

He leads me in the paths of righteousness
You are my Guide

For His name's sake
You are my Purpose

Yea, though I walk through the valley of the shadow of death
You are my Strength

I will fear no evil
You are my Security

For You are with me
You are my Peace

Your rod and your staff, they comfort me
You are my Deliverer

You prepare a table before me in the presence of my enemies
You are my Hope

You anoint my head with oil
You are my Blessing

My cup runs over
You are my Abundance

Surely goodness and mercy shall follow me all the days of my life
You are my Promise

And I will dwell in the house of the Lord
You are my Destiny

Forever
You are my All in All!

MARY SOUTHERLAND

Stress-Busters

From Ellen and Sally

Eat God-made foods for your God-made body. Fresh raw fruits and vegetables are filled with valuable nutrients. Eat organic when possible as organic means there are no man-made additives in those foods. Junk foods, especially those high in sugar, trans fats, caffeine, alcohol, and artificial additives, are serious stressors. A way to monitor the variety of nutrients in your Stress-Buster diet is to eat at least three different God-made colors at every meal.

○ ○ ○

- Clean house. It gives you a chance to work off steam while completing a task.

- I have learned great self-defense techniques, lost weight, and now get quality time with my 14-year-old son by taking a class with him. I can take out my frustrations on the bags and nobody gets hurt.

- Go to bed at the same time every night. Establish a routine to signal your mind and body that it's time to rest—like a cup of chamomile tea or a warm bath scented with lavender. In addition, make sure that your mattress is comfortable along with soft sheets in soothing shades.

- Learn to take one ten-minute power nap each day.

- Get organized. Plan, schedule, take notes, and keep good records. Use a calendar, computer software organizer, or write out a to-do list. Organizing the details of your daily life reduces stress. Save your memory for more creative and pleasurable activities.

- Do your most unpleasant or most difficult task at the beginning of the day when you are fresh. You'll avoid the stress of last-minute preparation. Procrastination feeds stress.

- If a task takes less than ten minutes to do…do it now. Otherwise, all of those little jobs will accumulate, creating a big stressor.

- Be realistic about what you can accomplish in a day. It's better to emphasize quality in your work, rather than sheer quantity. Careful planning prevents stress. Planning goals and objectives allows you to meet them more realistically. If you're new at goal setting, ask someone who is experienced for help.

- Scheduling stressful activities can reduce the number of stressors you must juggle at any one time. Don't set identical deadlines for major projects. Schedule some margins in each day that will allow you time for recharging and creative thinking. When the unexpected comes, you'll be better prepared.

- Take responsibility for your decisions. It's less stressful to make decisions and take action than to feel powerless and react to the decisions of others. Decide what you want and go for it. Always have a dream and goals for reaching that dream.

- Make a practice of throwing away or giving away one thing each day. Stuff can be a great stress producer.

- Eliminate financial debt. Create a budget and stick to it. Having a set financial plan eliminates financial stress.

I Say

I say: It is impossible.
God says: All things are possible (Luke 18:27).

I say: I am too tired.
God says: I will give you rest (Matthew 11:28-30).

I say: Nobody really loves me.
God says: I love you (John 3:16).

I say: I cannot go on.
God says: My grace is sufficient (2 Corinthians 12:9).

I say: I do not know which way to go.
God says: I will direct your steps (Proverbs 3:5-6).

I say: I will fail.
God says: You can do all things (Philippians 4:13).

I say: It is just not worth it.
God says: It will be worth it (Romans 8:28).

I say: I cannot forgive myself.
God says: I forgive you (1 John 1:9).

I say: I am in trouble.
God says: I will supply all your needs (Philippians 4:19).

I say: I am afraid.
God says: I have not given you a spirit of fear (2 Timothy 1:7).

I say: I am worried.
God says: Cast all your cares on Me (1 Peter 5:7).

AUTHOR UNKNOWN

3

Know When to Rest

He makes me to lie down in green pastures; He leads me beside
the still quiet waters. He restores my soul.
PSALM 23:2-3 NKJV

Jehovah-Rapha: *The Lord Who Heals*

~ The Shepherd and His Sheep ~

Sheep instinctively know that as long as they follow the shepherd, he will meet their needs, one of which is water. The shepherd always goes ahead of his sheep in order to find an ample supply of sweet green grass and refreshing water. He then leads the flock to the place where they can drink and eat. Even when they go through a dangerous valley, the shepherd is beside them. At the end of the day, the shepherd leads the flock back to the fold, a three-sided brush enclosure, and stands by the open door to examine each sheep as it enters. If the shepherd sees a sheep that's bruised or weary, he spreads refreshing oil on it to soothe and heal its wounds, and then he gives the sheep a drink of cool water. In short, sheep are completely helpless and totally dependent upon the shepherd.

○ ○ ○

I recently heard the frightening statistic that sleeping less than five hours produces the same response time as someone who is legally drunk. If that statement is true, I am in serious trouble because I rarely get more than five or six hours of sleep. I have always been a night person and have grown to cherish those precious, silent hours when the house is quiet. When I do climb into bed, sleep usually comes quickly—until the last few weeks. Insomnia is something new for me. I have come to dread the night and my silent but fierce battle with sleep. Tossing and turning and watching the hours creep by leaves a great deal of time to think, pray, and learn. I love the promise that "He gives to His beloved even in his sleep" (Psalm 127:2 NASB). I don't want to miss out on whatever God wants to give me in my sleep. I've tried everything from warm baths and warm milk to relaxation exercises and several herbal concoctions that were downright nasty. The sheep are counted and the blessings listed. I've solved several world problems, but what world leader would listen to a woman with dark circles under her eyes who finds it hard to put a complete sentence together due to sleep deprivation?

Then a wonderful thing happened. I got the flu! I know what you are thinking. Lack of sleep has made her crazy. True—but I was so sick that I was forced to see a doctor. During the course of her examination, she happened to ask how I was sleeping. Now, I'm certain she was not even remotely prepared for my response as frustration and exhaustion spilled out all over her nice, quiet office. Her eyes widened in surprise as I ranted and raved. When I finished my tirade, she smiled and quietly said, "Let's figure out what the problem is." Just like that. We talked for more than an hour about my life, the medications I was taking, and every ache, pain, and problem I was experiencing. After a thorough examination, she removed her glasses, sat down, and smiled that knowing smile that only doctors seem to possess. "I think I know what the problem is," she said.

Evidently, insomnia is a side effect of a new medication I am taking. It makes most people sleepy but, in my case, causes sleeplessness. She made some adjustments and prescribed a new medication. Last night I slept better than I have in months. I could not believe it. I didn't know whether to hug the doctor or deck her. Where had she been all of these sleepless weeks and why had she waited so long to figure out the problem? You already know where I'm going with this one. She had been there all along, waiting in her office for me, and holding the answer in her hand. Desperation made me seek her help. God's plan is not for us to stumble through the hours and days of life, exhausted and depleted to the point of desperation, drowning in stress. We can choose to rest. We can learn to be still.

> Come to me, all of you who are tired and have heavy loads, and I will give you rest. Accept my teachings and learn from me, because I am gentle and humble in spirit, and you will find rest for your lives (Matthew 11: 28-29 NCV).

Here I am, writing a book on stress. It seems I always have to relive a topic before I speak or write about it. (I think my next book will be *How to Become a Millionaire and Lose Thirty Pounds in Six Short Weeks*. Interestingly enough, I have had several offers to co-author.) Over the last several months, stress has camped out on my doorstep. Admittedly, it seems that a helicopter is always landing somewhere in my life, but these last few months have exceeded my wildest stress-filled expectations and have, I suspect, something to do with the fact that I'm writing this book. How has stress bombarded my life? Let me count the ways.

It started out innocently enough when our daughter's boyfriend gave her two male cats as a gift. Both cats had litters of kittens within a month of each other, which meant, at one point, that we had nine kittens. Keeping the litters separated and away from our two dogs required diligent monitoring, during which time I had a month-long battle with viral meningitis. We pursued, located, contacted, and met our adopted daughter's birth mother. My husband's parents came for a visit, during which my mother-in-law had emergency surgery for a perforated ulcer, was in the hospital for 11 days, and was with us for six weeks while recovering. I was sick with bronchitis. My West Highland Terrier, Scruffy, was poisoned by someone who fed her bread soaked with antifreeze. Our son's college football team won their conference championship, which meant that each weekend was occupied with out-of-town football games. My husband was sick with bronchitis. My publisher reminded me that they were looking forward to reading a 60,000-word manuscript I had agreed to write. Dan's father was sick with bronchitis. Dan underwent several cardio-versions, an out-patient procedure during which he is placed under general anesthesia and hooked up to wires resembling jumper cables, through which an electric current flows, shocking his heart back into a normal rhythm. The Thanksgiving holidays came and went. I got bronchitis…again. The Christmas holidays came and went, during which our son rescued and brought home a stray puppy, meaning that we again have two dogs and nine cats. We put our house on the market in an effort to downsize and eliminate debt. Our son, Jered, was in a wreck that totaled his truck, but thankfully left him and his girlfriend uninjured. Our daughter, Danna, had what the doctor called "the worst case of mononucleosis" he had ever seen, resulting in three visits to the emergency room. My husband and I, along with several other couples, launched a new church that is exploding in growth. Dan went into cardiac arrest, resulting in a nine-day hospital stay and the insertion of a defibrillator. Get the picture?

We cannot negotiate the existence of stress. We simply have to learn how to manage it, and one of the most important steps in managing stress is learning how to be still and rest. As parents, how many times have we issued the command to "be still"? My children have been the recipients of that decree more often than I care to remember. The truth is, they take after their mother when it comes to being still—or should I say *not* being still. Furthermore, I have inadvertently conveyed the message that to be still is to be useless and unproductive, a truth that was recently brought home to me by our 19-year-old daughter.

To say that I spend a great deal of time at my computer is like saying that the sun comes up each morning. In my defense, a great deal of my job and ministry responsibilities are done through our home office. Every writing assignment and book manuscript is done on my computer. Online Bible studies, newsletters, resource orders, prayer requests, responses to e-mails, and website updates make up a great deal of the day-to-day management of Journey Ministry and all of it is orchestrated from my desk.

One of the things that I love most about Danna is her desire to share the minute details of her life with me. When she hits the door, she always has a story to tell and heads straight to the sofa in my office to find her audience. I am usually there. However, last week, the walls of the office began to close in and the whining began pouring out of my mind and heart. "I am never writing another book!" I promised myself and God. "I'm sick and tired of putting words together in sentences!" I moaned. "My back hurts from sitting at this ridiculous desk." Enough! I needed a break and headed for our screened-in porch to play with kittens and watch the leaves change colors.

I heard Danna come in and knew exactly where she was going— to the study. Silence was followed by the sound of footsteps across the living room, through the kitchen, through my bedroom, and into my bathroom. More silence. I wondered how long it would take her to find me. I then realized just how sad it was that the first two places my daughter thought to look for her mom were the study and the bathroom. As I pondered that pathetic realization, Danna burst through the door, a look of relief on her beautiful face. "Mom, are you okay?" she gasped. A fresh realization slammed into my mind and heart. My life obviously preached the loud message that rest is sin and that if I am sitting still, something must be wrong. I tried to dress that realization up and make it look and sound better, but the ugly and blatant truth remained. Obviously, I'm not an expert when it comes to the subject of rest. In fact, I have met few people who are. It is time for me to surrender, sit at God's feet, listen to His voice, and rest. Join me.

Rest Is Not an Option

A friend recently told me the story of a young mother attending church with her five-year-old daughter. As the congregation stood to sing the chorus, "I Exalt Thee, O Lord..." the mother glanced down at her daughter to see her little arms up in the air as she sang, "I'm exhausted, O Lord..." I can relate.

Let me be perfectly honest. So far, I have spent more time on this chapter than any other part of this book. There's a very good reason. I am *terrible* at this "rest" thing, forever walking the thin line between being productive and my life spiraling out of control. When I asked friends and prayer warriors to pray for me as I worked on a manuscript entitled *Escaping the Stress Trap*, they invariably burst into laughter. I did not appreciate their attitudes.

I've repeatedly tried to defy my God-given need for rest, thinking that I'm somehow "above" both the occurrence and consequences of exhaustion. Some urgent task will always call my name, as will that person whose life will absolutely disintegrate before my eyes if I don't do something right now. Stress shouts, "Get busy! There's so much to do!" Stress applauds and dances with delight as I keep on "doing" instead of "being."

Stress can make us sick and, according to medical experts, stress is deadly. Between 60 to 90 percent of all medical patients complain about stress-related symptoms. My doctor tells me that stress can be good or bad, but either way, stress takes its toll. The psalmist writes, "He lets me rest" (Psalm 23:2 NLT). Don't allow that gentle statement to fool you. The Revised Standard Version of the Bible says it this way, "He makes me lie down in green pastures." I can personally testify to the fact that the word "makes" holds a world of possibilities from God's hand at work in my life and have come to the conclusion that, make no mistake, we will rest—one way or another.

Throughout the years God has gently grabbed my attention with an illness that drove me to bed or a crisis that drove me to my knees. He is a persistent, loving Father and well aware of just how much we need to rest and how much rest we need. The loving hand of God tucked the need for rest into our physical being during the creation process.

On the seventh day of creation, God rested. That has always amazed me! Did He *need* to rest? Obviously not, but He drove home the eternal fact that our bodies were created in such a way that rest is not really an option—our need to rest is a physical and spiritual reality.

Rest Heals and Restores

> He [Elijah] went on alone into the desert, traveling all day. He sat down under a solitary broom tree [juniper tree] and prayed that he might die. "I have had enough, LORD," he said. "Take my life, for I am no better than my ancestors." Then he lay down and slept under the broom tree. But as he was sleeping, an angel touched him and told him, "Get up and eat!" He looked around and saw some bread baked on hot stones and a jar of water! So he ate and drank and lay down again. Then the angel of the LORD came again and touched him and said, "Get up and eat some more, for there is a long journey ahead of you." So he got up and ate and drank, and the food gave him enough strength to travel forty days and forty nights to Mount Sinai, the mountain of God (1 Kings 19:4-8 NLT).

Elijah is a great example of good stress gone bad. One day he was the conquering hero, the next we find him sitting under a juniper tree, feeling sorry for himself and begging God to let him die. The poor man was simply exhausted. True, it was an exhaustion produced by victory, but it was still exhaustion. Elijah had called down fire from heaven, proving the existence of the only true God, destroying idols and idol worshippers (1 Kings 18:19-40). Big stuff! In fact, it's my personal opinion that he should have been celebrating. So why was he so discouraged? Because of a woman, Jezebel, who was largely responsible for his discouragement. Jezebel was furious. When she learned what had happened on Mount Carmel with the fire and idols, she put a contract out on Elijah (1 Kings 19:2). Now, stop and think about that for a moment. Elijah had been in the presence of God. God had heard and answered Elijah's prayer, putting on a fiery display for all to see. Idols had fallen. The prophets of Baal had either fled or been destroyed. And Elijah is worried about one angry woman?

Great discouragement often follows great victory. Battle consumes energy and often leaves the warrior depleted and exhausted. Have you noticed that stress and exhaustion always produce skewed perspectives? Elijah had lost his perspective and was ready to quit, which is where we find him...collapsed under a juniper tree with the spoils of fresh victory all but forgotten. God's solution was simple. Elijah needed rest. Elijah slept and ate and then slept some more. It's interesting to note that the juniper tree was common to the desert. So is stress. Deserts are filled with stress and exhaustion. Elijah stayed in the desert for 40 days, not because he had been disobedient or sinned, but because he was stressed out and needed time to rest. God replenished and restored him there.

A visitor saw several shepherds in Nazareth bringing their flocks to water them at the well. When the sheep had drunk their fill, the shepherds called and their sheep immediately followed. The visitor asked the shepherds if the sheep always followed their own shepherds when they called. "Yes," said one of the shepherds, "under one condition. The sheep that don't follow the voice of their shepherd are the sick sheep. If a sheep is healthy, it will always follow its shepherd, but if there is something wrong with the sheep, it will follow anybody."

When we are sick and exhausted, we are in danger of following the wrong voice. Our defenses are down and our discernment is dulled by the stress of life. Rest heals and restores.

Rest Encourages Obedience

My husband is the master of the ten-minute nap. Dan Southerland can sleep anywhere. It used to make me so angry when I would walk—no, run—through the living room and see my husband taking a nap. What a waste of time! He could be doing so many more important and spiritual things with those ten minutes. It took a two-year-battle with clinical depression to understand that rest is a command from God, a built-in need, and something meant for our good. Who knows us better than the One who created us?

Fatigue is not one of the spiritual gifts, yet we proudly wear our dark-circled and sleep-deprived eyes as badges of honor and sacrificial living. The enemy loves that. If he can keep us exhausted, he is confident we will be no threat to him. We must learn to rest.

We must also learn *when* we need to rest. I have discovered an irritating truth. We need to rest most when we have the least amount of time to rest. I hate that! I hate the fact that God calls me away from my vicious circle of religious activity and into His presence. After all, I spent a lot of time getting all of those irons in the fire. But every time I obey His call to "come apart," He transforms that "ineffective" activity into powerful, life-transforming relationship with Him lived out in a life of purpose and passion.

The human body is programmed for a certain amount of rest. We can cheat it short-term, but not long-term. Rest affects the efficiency rating of this human body in which we dwell and increases productivity. Rest is replenishing. While we sleep and rest, the Father repairs and restores. We run on batteries that must be recharged daily. I've discovered that when I'm tired, it's much harder for me to handle stress. Just as 90 percent of income goes further when we tithe ten percent of it, so does our energy when we tithe it in rest.

We only have one physical body with no trade-ins or exchanges. If God keeps track of the number of hairs on our head (Luke 12:7), then He's certainly concerned about our physical welfare. Someone recently sent me an e-mail entitled, "To Exercise or Not to Exercise—That's the Question":

1. I have to exercise early in the morning before my brain figures out what I am doing.

2. If God meant for us to touch our toes, He would have put them further up our body.

3. The advantage of exercising every day is that you die healthier.

4. I don't jog—it makes the ice jump right out of my glass.

5. I joined a health club last year, spent about $400, and haven't lost a pound. Apparently, you have to show up.

In a serious attempt to become physically fit, the Southerlands joined a local gym that offers a special family rate. It's quite a place. Hundreds of machines designed to stretch and pull every muscle in the human body occupy three levels of this beautiful facility. Classes of all kinds teach you how to jump, spin, dance, and step the pounds off. Massage therapists work their magic, soothing those newly stretched muscles that are rebelliously sore. Steam rooms, saunas, hot tubs, and heated pools are available as well as a refreshment bar, where smiling, disgustingly toned employees offer to mix a protein power smoothie just for you. Yum! Personal trainers are available to design an individualized program that will help you meet your individual fitness goals. They weigh, measure, and coach you through those first painful days. You can see that absolutely everything we need to lose weight and become physically fit is ready and waiting for us at this gym. All we need is the discipline to go.

> Do you not know that your body is a temple of the Holy Spirit, who is in you, whom you have received from God? You are not your own; you were bought at a price. Therefore, honor God with your body (1 Corinthians 6:19-20).

We simply cannot give our hearts to God and keep our bodies for ourselves. The body is a temple that houses the Holy Spirit as well as our mind, heart, and emotions. When disobedience reigns here—in the physical body—it becomes a toehold for failure, defeat, and stress.

Rest Is Productive

For most of my adult life, I have wrongly equated being busy with being productive. I'm guilty as charged when it comes to living each day in overdrive. My Day-Timer has, at times, been my Bible. The result has always been exhaustion, burnout, and watered-down living. Everything looked great on the outside—but when I was alone, just God and me, we both knew the facade I had so carefully erected was a spiritual monument to self-promotion and pride-filled goals. The house built upon the sand seemed like very familiar digs. And I was not alone.

We are all masters of rationalizing our way to approval. The problem is that the approval we gain comes from impotent and lifeless sources. I am convinced that if we are willing to surrender our lives to the tyranny of the urgent, the enemy will keep the urgent things in life coming—people who need you immediately, those who clamor for your attention above your family and personal relationship with God, the person who can talk to no one but you, and the list goes on. What ego strokes they offer! And what futility.

I have always loved music and began taking piano lessons at the age of five. I will never forget that first piano lesson with Mrs. McKenzie, a very sweet, elderly woman who played the piano beautifully. Her hair was slightly blue, her house smelled like lemon drops, and she had clocks that chimed every 15 minutes. I was so excited and ready to play the piano like my sister, who played for our church worship services. Betty was amazing, and I was desperately hoping that same musical ability ran in our family. "Let's get started," Mrs. McKenzie said.

I climbed up on the piano bench, waiting for her brilliant instruction to begin. She placed a bright red piano book in front of me and invited me to open it to the first page. I was disappointed to see only little black pictures. Where was the music? Where were the songs? Mrs. McKenzie smiled as she patiently began to explain the musical symbols pictured in the book before me. I soon grew restless. "What's wrong, Mary?" she asked. "I want to play the piano, please," I softly responded. With a knowing smile, she said, "We'll get to that." I was not happy.

On and on—it seemed like hours—Mrs. McKenzie pointed to funny-shaped black symbols, named them, and explained their meaning. I was not impressed. I just wanted to get my hands on that keyboard. Sensing my impatience, Mrs. McKenzie pointed to one of the symbols on the page before me and said, "Mary, this small black box is called a 'rest' and is one of the most important symbols in music." I simply didn't care. It did nothing but sit on a page in useless and unproductive silence. I wanted music. "Do you know why rests are so important in music?" she persisted. Obviously, I had no clue until she said something I remember to this day, "The music that comes after the rest is the most beautiful music of all." I didn't understand the deeper meaning of those words then, but life and time have since illustrated their importance and their truth. The best part of life comes after we rest in Him. The most beautiful service follows time spent at His feet. Rest is a powerful part of our life song. The rest in music prepares the listener for what comes next. So does rest in life.

Rest Empowers Solitude

Solitude and rest go hand in hand. Solitude is one of God's best stress-busters and a powerful discipline in the life of a disciple. To be alone with and before God brings power that can be found in no other place. At His feet, listening and waiting, is where we begin to understand the daily reality of a purpose-filled life. It's in His arms that we are bathed in unconditional love, transformed and equipped to live an abundant life. Failure to practice solitude often leads to burnout, exhaustion, and a frantic, stress-filled existence lived on the run. We are His sheep, and sheep are never fully at ease around rushing water. The Shepherd leads His sheep beside still waters. The reason is very simple.

Sheep instinctively know that the weight of their wool, when wet, will drown them. Sheep need still, quiet waters in order to live—and so do we. The psalmist offers a foundational truth when he writes, "Be still, and know that I am God" (Psalm 46:10). This verse implies there is much about God we cannot know on the run. It also suggests that when we do carve out time with Him alone and are still before Him, we will know Him more.

I'm not certain that a hit-and-run type of life can really be called living. Undoubtedly, Jesus didn't live this way while on earth. In fact, His times of solitude and rest are clearly recorded in Scripture. Solitude not only replenishes us for life, it provides the place we can and must go in order to know Him intimately. Stillness implies quietness and solitude, the place where our minds grow clear and our souls catch up.

The more responsibility we carry and the busier we are, the more we need regular solitude. There is a Greek motto that says it well, "You will break the bow if you keep it always bent." How many people break under the load of stress because there is no solitude in their schedules? We need to unbend by secluding ourselves with God. If we don't schedule solitude, it will rarely, if ever, happen. We plan and schedule the things in life we deem important, often missing the highest things from God's hand. Stress thrives on chaos and frenzy. Solitude, time spent in His presence just listening and being, is a place where we are empowered and equipped for life, the place where stress is disarmed and peace reigns. What steps can we take in order to make solitude a regular part of our daily lives?

Step One: Recognize the Value of Solitude

Four years ago my family and I moved from South Florida to Charlotte, North Carolina, a place we have grown to love. The change of seasons, rolling hills, and Southern hospitality gently drew us in and made it home. Our house sits on a beautiful lot, and our backyard is filled with tall trees and a wide variety of birds. Now, I must admit that I have never been a bird-watcher, but I soon decided that a couple of bird feeders were definitely called for. It was an experiment of sorts. I pictured small delicately feathered creatures congregating in our backyard to provide beauty and entertainment for our family and friends. Instead, I got large colorless birds that ate huge amounts of seed and grew fatter each day. Pigeons! I got pigeons! They swooped into my birdhouses and pranced in my grass as if to say, "I am here to stay, honey! Get used to it!" I didn't like their attitude, but what I did find fascinating about these feathered intruders was their awkward walk.

I watched the pigeons, day in and day out, wondering what God had in mind when He created these comical birds. I headed for my computer, determined to solve this feathered mystery. I soon learned that a pigeon walks the way it does so it can see where it's going. It seems that the pigeon's eyes can't adjust their focus as the bird moves, so it actually has to bring its head to a complete stop between steps in order to refocus. As a result, the pigeon must walk with its head forward, stop, head back, stop.

We can learn an important truth from these amusing birds. We need to build into our lives a pattern of "stops" called solitude. My dictionary defines solitude as "detachment, separation, or disconnection." Solitude is when we deliberately separate and detach ourselves from the momentum of our daily schedule in order to refocus and determine where we really are headed and what really is important. One of the reasons that solitude is so hard to come by is that we live in a world that desperately tries to avoid it. Yet solitude is one of our basic needs and wisest disciplines. Recognizing the value of solitude is a first step toward making it a regular part of our lives.

Solitude Helps Us Pray

Early the next morning, while it was still dark, Jesus woke

and left the house. He went to a lonely place, where he prayed (Mark 1:35 NCV).

Time spent alone with God—praying—enables us to hear and recognize His voice above the noise of life. Jesus often got alone to pray. He even left ministry situations to practice solitude. People were flocking to hear Him preach and to have their diseases healed, but He made sure He often withdrew to quiet, solitary places to pray. It was a spiritual habit.

Many things clamor for our attention, and we often run ourselves ragged attending to each one. Like Jesus, however, we should take time to withdraw to a quiet and deserted place to pray. Strength comes from God alone. In His presence, at His feet, is the place of power.

Solitude Helps Us Resist Sin

Be angry, and do not sin. Meditate within your heart on your bed and be still (Psalm 4:4 NKJV).

Temptation is the first step on the road to sin. As my husband often says, you cannot keep a bird from flying over your head, but you can certainly keep it from building a nest in your hair. In other words, temptation will come. Although temptation originates in human desire, it can be stopped if we learn how to resist and control those desires.

While speaking for a conference in Sterling, Colorado, my daily ride on the winding country roads to the conference center took me past field after field of cows. One morning, I spotted a sign that read "If you hit a cow, you pay for the cow." A local farmer explained that cows often escape and get lost. When I asked how a cow could possibly get lost, he said, "Well, the cow starts nibbling on a patch of green grass. When it finishes, it looks ahead to the next patch of grass and starts nibbling on that one. Then it nibbles on a clump of grass right next to a hole in the fence. On the other side of the fence is another patch of grass, which the cow nibbles. The next thing you know the cow has nibbled itself right into being lost." Sin is usually not one big bite of rebellion but the result of many small nibbles. Eve chose to give in to rather than control her natural desires and physical appetites. "When the woman saw that the fruit of the tree was good for food and pleasing to the eye, and also desirable for gaining wisdom, she took some and ate it. She also gave some to her husband, who was with her, and he ate it" (Genesis 3:6).

We are tempted the way Eve was tempted. When she ate that fruit, it was more than just a rebellious act. It was choosing to value her own desires over God's will. It was choosing to believe the lies of Satan. Adam was just as guilty as Eve—not just because he ate the fruit, but because he said nothing. Self-control is the choice to do the right thing in preparation for facing temptation. Time spent in prayerful solitude strengthens us for the war with temptation. Stress lowers our defenses and often distracts us from what is right and true, while solitude strengthens our awareness of the enemy's schemes.

Solitude Helps Us Withstand Trials

> On my bed I remember you; I think of you through the watches of the night. Because you are my help, I sing in the shadow of your wings (Psalm 63:6-7).

Solitude reminds us that we can trust God. Southerland vacations always begin with "the plan." Before we pack even one sock or book one hotel room, the Southerlands are summoned to a family meeting with one item on the agenda—a discussion of the current vacation plan. Everyone has the opportunity to make suggestions and share ideas. Dan and I then pool those ideas and make a final decision. Once the destination is chosen, Dan goes to work, charting every stop, logging the number of miles between stops, booking hotel rooms when we can't take any more stops, and locating child-friendly restaurants along the way. While living in South Florida, one of our favorite vacation spots could usually be found nestled somewhere in the Smoky Mountains of North Carolina, where we now live. Dan couldn't wait to pack up our faithful old van, plug in the country music, and hit the road. He claimed that just this side of the North Carolina state line he could actually smell those Blue Ridge Mountains.

Over the years every family member discovered a different reason for loving North Carolina. I was drawn to the quaint little towns filled with that winsome country charm, smiling people, and picturesque antique stores. Dan loved the winding mountain roads and slower pace of life, while our two children clamored to stop and play in the icy mountain water of every stream or creek they saw. Their all-time favorite spot was Sliding Rock, a gigantic boulder that has been transformed into a huge water slide by the powerful falls above it. Our first experience at Sliding Rock—when Jered was five and Danna was two—proved to be quite an event.

Wiggling out of my arms, Jered ran straight to the rock and hurriedly plopped down, squealing with delight as the chilly rushing water carried him over the frozen slab and into the icy pool at the bottom. Danna just watched, her big brown eyes wide with questioning fear as she witnessed her brother's disappearance down the mountain. When Jered's curly head popped out of the water, Danna's face flooded with relief as she clapped and cheered for "Bubba." Dan was next, whooping and hollering Texas style as he catapulted down the watery slide. Coming up for air, he made his way back to the top of the rock, held out his arms, and shouted, "Danna! Come with me!"

Now my daughter didn't fully comprehend *what* was being asked of her but she undoubtedly recognized *who* was doing the asking—her daddy. To my utter and total amazement, our usually tentative, fearful daughter rushed into the outstretched and familiar arms of her father, tightly clutching his hands as he positioned her in his frozen lap. Down they went! I waited and wondered at the outcome. When they popped up out of the frigid pool Danna was laughing, sputtering, and begging, "We do it again, Daddy! We do it again!" She didn't understand the plan, but she knew and trusted the "plan maker." So can we.

Solitude Strengthens Us

> Blessed is the man who does not walk in the counsel of the wicked or stand in the way of sinners or sit in the seat of mockers. But his delight is in the law of the Lord, and on his law he meditates day and night. He is like a tree planted by streams of water, which yields its fruit in season and whose leaf does not wither. Whatever he does prospers (Psalm 1:1-3).

Most of us tend to think of silence as empty and hollow instead of full and rich. We fill our lives, homes, and hearts with noise and activity in order to avoid silence at all costs. So much of God is realized in stillness. The enemy stands against time spent in solitude because Satan knows the power waiting for us in those tranquil moments, the quiet moments. We must carve out time for solitude and wage battle in order to protect it. The reality is that if we don't "come apart," we will come apart.

The seasons of silence are different in nature and purpose. Sometimes silence falls like a sweet, gentle, and refreshing rain. During those times, I am meeting the One I love the most...and just reveling in His presence. I don't have to do anything or be anything other than His chosen child. I'm with Him and He's with me. I crawl up into His lap, wrap my arms around Him as He holds me fast, and just stay for awhile. During these silent times He brings healing and restoration. New strength comes as I fall in love with Him all over again and He reminds me that His love is unchanging, unconditional, and faithful. "I am not going anywhere," He promises.

Then there are times when the silence is like a deep, dark pit. Several years ago, I went through a two-year clinical depression that still nips at my heels every moment of every day. But in that dark pit, I found the life-changing promises of Psalm 40:1-3:

> I waited patiently for the LORD; he turned to me and heard

my cry. He lifted me out of the slimy pit, out of the mud and mire; he set my feet on a rock and gave me a firm place to stand. He put a new song in my mouth, a hymn of praise to our God. Many will see and fear and put their trust in the LORD.

Oh, I had read the book of Psalms many times and had even taught a series of lessons based on the psalms. This time, in the silence, the reality of His promises settled into my soul and took root. I learned how to wait on God…how to cry out to Him…how to trust Him like the helpless child I am while He first delivered me *in* that pit and then *from* that pit, firmly planting my feet on the rock of His truth. I learned how to practice joy, not just feel it. He taught me that I'm His and His alone, and that He is a very possessive parent. A wonderful, horrible pit totally changed my very being, redefined my identity, and set the direction of my life journey. The most powerful, effective ministry of my life has come *after* that pit experience.

Step Two: Choose to Practice Solitude

After weeks of tests, the doctor looked at me and said, "Mary, there is nothing wrong with you except for the fact that you don't know how to deal with stress. You'd better learn how or it will kill you." My first thought was, *What a rude man! He obviously does not understand that I'm a pastor's wife who tells people how to deal with their stress.* He then handed me a magazine article entitled "Seven Steps to a Stress-Free Life." A quick glance told me that the steps were nothing more than the same old, tired suggestions that I'd seen, read, and even taught. As my anger and frustration grew, God whispered to my frantic heart, "Mary, you know what to do." The silence that followed His words swelled with an unspoken but powerful conviction that my problem was not that I didn't know what to do. The problem was that I was not doing what I knew. Last time I checked, God called that sin (James 4:17).

The choice to practice solitude is a choice to obey God. God always honors obedience. When we make the commitment to practice solitude, the Father not only empowers that commitment, but also provides everything we need to keep it, including circumstances that drive us to the end of ourselves and to the point of desperation.

Every season of silence is pregnant with possibilities that have been strained through God's hands. I wouldn't trade the silent times for anything because it is in those times that He whispers, "I adore you...no matter what you do or don't do. You are the apple of My eye. I will never leave you. You are never alone. You really do matter and your life really is counting in the kingdom. You are important to me. I have a plan!" I take every pain, every hurt, and every disappointment this world inflicts, friends who disappoint me and children who break my heart, my own constant sin, and ask Him what I'm supposed to do with them. When victory comes, I rush into His waiting embrace, shouting, "Look, Abba Father, Dearest Daddy! Is this cool or what?" His arms immediately pull me against His heart and we have what my kids call "Daddy time." We laugh, we cry, and we talk about the trials that brought me there. I am always reminded that anyone or anything that makes me cry out to Him, any circumstance that drives me into His arms, can be counted as good.

I am learning to embrace the silent times as a gift instead of a trial. Time under the juniper tree is good. Sometimes I just need to be reminded of that.

Stress-Busters

From Ellen and Sally

Relax. Be still. Listen. Know God will provide. He created an earth filled with peaceful nature to soothe our souls. He gave us the desire, need, and physical mechanisms to sleep. He also created foods to calm our minds and bodies. Be still and listen to your Father. Prayer is God's highway for communication with you.

Sleep. Be still for no less than 6 to 8 hours. Sleep deprivation is a major cause of mental and physical stress. For a good night's sleep, avoid snacks before bedtime, especially sugar and grains. Complete darkness prevents a disruption in your circadian rhythms. Sorry, no TV right before bed as it's too stimulating for the brain. So are mystery and suspense novels. For peaceful, rejuvenating sleep, read the Bible.

Nap. A 15-minute nap mid-afternoon will rejuvenate and refresh you for the rest of the day. Set a timer.

Eat. God created certain foods that calm the nervous system. Avocadoes, green beans, broccoli, leafy greens, spinach, sweet potatoes, parsley, blueberries, raspberries, figs, pineapple, almonds, walnuts, flaxseeds, sesame seeds, chickpeas, oats, brown rice, fish oils, olive oil, goat cheese, mozzarella cheese, ricotta cheese, plain yogurt, eggs, chicken, turkey, lamb, lean beef, salmon and chlorella top an impressive list.

Think. Know that you are not powerless. Have confidence in your problem-solving abilities and in your God. Keep things in perspective. Choose to major on the major things and minor on the minor things. Live in the present where you have control. Accept the difference in individuals, knowing that you can only change yourself.

Move. A brisk ten-minute walk will do wonders for your stress level. Stretching will be especially helpful in relaxing. Exercise from a viewpoint of obedience. Walk on the beach…a country road…in your neighborhood.

○ ○ ○

- I find one moment in the day that I consciously recognize as beautiful.

- I love to sit and watch the clouds. This puts me in a totally different frame of mind and the stress I'm experiencing vanishes.

- Take a hot bath, complete with candles and soft music. Adding Epsom salts will naturally relax your muscles and reduce stress.

- Get a massage. Since a professional massage can be costly, check to see if you have a physical therapy school in your area. After completing all course work, students must have a certain number of hours in giving massages before they receive their degree. You can sometimes get an hour-long massage for as little as $10.

- Divide large tasks into a series of small tasks that are more manageable.

- I've taken up knitting and crocheting. It keeps my hands and mind busy and I can't eat while I'm doing it, so no "pigging out!" I have the added benefit of making Christmas presents I think people appreciate!

- Rub warm lotion on your hands and feet. Massage each area, using your thumbs to apply pressure while rubbing in small circles.

- Buy a punching bag. When angry or stressed out, put on boxing gloves and spend 30 minutes punching that bag. Can't afford a punching bag? A bed works just as well.

- Go to the water. The sound of waves or a bubbling stream is calming and a proven stress reliever.

- Take the first five minutes of the morning to stretch, move gently, and focus on the day ahead. Ask God to guide your steps and give you His peace.

4

Do What God Gives You to Do

He leads me in paths of righteousness for His name's sake.
PSALM 23:3 NKJV

Jehovah-Tsidkenu: *The Lord Our Righteousness*

~ The Shepherd and His Sheep ~

Living among their sheep all day, sleeping among them at night, the shepherd becomes a friend to the sheep as they do to him. Each sheep has its own name and will come at once when it is called. They understand the warning cry of danger, and come running to their shepherd for protection. They know their shepherd's voice so well that when several flocks have been mixed up together at a watering place or in a fold where it would seem impossible to sort them out, the shepherds take different positions outside the flocks, each calling his own sheep. When the sheep hear their own shepherd's voice, they run to him. Without the leadership of the shepherd, they are doomed. The shepherd stands in front of his sheep, speaking softly,

81

motioning for them to follow him. The shepherd never leaves his sheep alone and has, in fact, already gone before the sheep to prepare the way ahead. In reality, sheep are simply doing what their shepherd has given them to do.

○ ○ ○

After my father's death, my mother worked three jobs to support our family while attending nursing school, something she had always wanted to do. I can still see her, cooking dinner, a textbook in one hand and a spatula in the other. After passing her nurse's exam, mother went to work at the local hospital in the small Texas town where we lived. Over time, she worked in several areas of the hospital, but her favorite spot, by far, was the nursery. Eventually she became a pediatric nurse.

Mother was wonderful with the babies and seemed to know just what they needed when no one else did. One fussy infant immediately calmed down and went to sleep when mother put a small transistor radio, tuned to soft, classical music, in the bassinet with the baby. She insisted on having rockers in the nursery so the babies could be rocked by volunteers. I decided I wanted to be a nurse just like her and promptly enrolled in the candy striper program offered by the high school I attended. When I told Mother the good news, she simply said, "That's wonderful, honey. You'll make a great nurse."

On my first day as a candy striper, I eagerly donned the red-and-white striped uniform and reported for duty. The head nurse welcomed me and explained that I would be checking with each patient to make sure they had water to drink, magazines to read, and a listening ear. Simple enough. "Oh, and one more thing," she continued. In retrospect, I should have instantly recognized the danger in those words and run for the nearest exit. In my ignorance, I stayed, Nurse Mary in the making. "Since we are shorthanded,

I may ask you to do just a few things to help the other nurses on duty," she said. "No problem," I assured her.

At that precise moment, a scream pierced the air! The head nurse calmly looked at me, smiled, and said, "Could you check on that, please?" Surely I had misunderstood her. "Now!" she continued. Taking a deep breath, I headed in the direction of the scream, praying that someone was just watching an exciting football game. No such luck.

As I neared the room in question, a bedpan flew through the doorway in front of me, landing at my feet. Furthermore, the bedpan was not empty! I decided right then and there that nursing was *not* for me, turned in my candy cane apron, and raced for the elevator. My mother was waiting as I stepped off of it. She smiled, handed me the cars keys, and said, "See you at home." Fortunately, I had a wonderful mother who knew me well, understood that I could never be a nurse, and encouraged me to be the teacher God had created me to be.

I truly believe many people are living stress-filled lives because they have never discovered God's plan and are trapped in jobs and careers that simply do not fit. Every day they feel like the proverbial round peg being jammed into a square hole. What does fit is God's plan. In Psalm 23:3, David writes, "He leads me in paths of righteousness" (NKJV). "Righteousness" simply means the "right things." The Shepherd has an agenda for His sheep. Unfortunately, so does everyone else. The difference is that God's agenda is filled with the "right things" He shaped and created us to do while the agendas of others service their own purpose instead of God's. The Shepherd empowers His agenda alone. Paul writes in 1 Thessalonians 5:24 that "faithful is He who calls you, and He also will bring it to pass" (NASB). In other words, God only empowers us to do what He shaped us to do. When we step into our own agenda or one created by anyone else, we are stepping into and relying upon our frail, limited strength. Soon we will be empty and stress will flood in, filling the emptiness with anxiety and tension.

I am amazed by the number of people who are drowning in the pit of unrealistic expectations imposed by others or themselves, exhausted by a life powered by human abilities and strength. Stress saturates every moment of every day, setting them up to fail. Marriages crumble and hearts shatter under the pressure of a life ordered by man instead of by God. I encourage you to find your spiritual gifts and use them. God takes pleasure in watching us "be" us as we do what He gives us to do. We were created in response to a unique, God-shaped plan; what we do for a living is an important part of that plan. While it is true that the "paths of righteousness" apply to our spiritual journey, it is just as true that they apply to our daily journey as well—which ultimately is our spiritual journey. Stress comes when we forget who our true audience is and end up doing wrong things dictated by others instead of doing the right things God planned for us to do. One of those right things is our work.

A woman was on the job when the babysitter called to tell her that her daughter was very sick. The woman quickly left work. On her way home, she dashed into a local pharmacy to pick up some medicine for her sick child. When she came out of the pharmacy, she discovered that she had locked her keys in the car. The woman frantically called home, only to hear that her daughter was worse. Looking around for help, she spotted an old rusty coat hanger lying on the ground. The woman picked it up but had no idea how to use it. By this time she was in a panic. Bowing her head, the anxious mother prayed for help. Just then an old rusty car pulled up. Out of the driver's seat emerged a dirty, greasy, bearded man wearing an old biker skull rag on his head. The woman was desperate, so she decided to be thankful for answered prayer. The man took the hanger, and in less than a minute, opened the car. Ecstatic with relief, the lady hugged her rescuer and through tears of joy said, "Thank you so much! You are a very nice man!" Embarrassed, the man replied, "Lady, I'm not a nice man. I've been in prison for car theft and just got out an hour ago." The woman hugged the man again and sobbed, "Thank You, God, for sending me a professional!"

We all want to be successful in our work. Your office may be downtown or just inside your front door. Your work clothes may be an elegant suit or ragged jeans and a stained T-shirt. You may be paid in cash or with crayon drawings and sticky kisses. It doesn't really matter because none of these things alone makes us successful in the workplace. Success in the workplace is not determined by *where* we work. It is determined by *how* we work.

The Proverbs 31 woman often gets a bad rap and is sometimes misunderstood. I've heard Bible teachers use this woman's life as the basis for their argument that a woman's place is *only* in the home when, in reality, the Proverbs 31 woman was a successful businesswoman at ease in her own skin and with her whole God-ordained identity. The life of this woman offers valuable principles that, when applied, will result in a purpose-driven life of doing the right things God has for us to do.

> She selects wool and flax and works with eager hands. She is like the merchant ships, bringing her food from afar. She gets up while it is still dark; she provides food for her family and portions for her servant girls. She considers a field and buys it; out of her earnings she plants a vineyard. She sets about her work vigorously; her arms are strong for her tasks (Proverbs 31:13-17).

Principle One: Choose Your Work Carefully

> She selects wool and flax (Proverbs 31:13).

God is the source of every skill, gift, ability, and talent we possess, and He wants us to use them to the best of our ability. Proverbs 22:6 encourages parents to "train a child in the way he should go, and when he is old he will not turn from it." "The way he should go" means in the ways of God and in the direction the child was created to go. In other words, we are designed with an inclination that draws us toward God and the plan He has for us to live out.

When our son was a baby and began to walk at the age of ten

months, I immediately noticed that his feet turned inward. Dan and I were very concerned and made an appointment for Jered to see an orthopedic specialist. After a thorough examination and several sets of X-rays, the doctor called us into his office. We braced ourselves for bad news but were relieved to hear him say, "There's nothing wrong with Jered's feet." Seeing the questioning look on my face, he continued. "Jered simply has the feet of a natural athlete, which is why he is pigeon-toed. His feet are designed to give him great balance."

Over the years, Jered's natural abilities have fueled his avid love for sports as he has played softball, soccer, basketball, and football. Consequently, he now attends an excellent, private, and expensive college on a full athletic and academic scholarship. Without that scholarship, we would never have been able to afford the tuition. His feet were part of God's plan. Go, God! Jered is not only receiving a top-shelf education, but he is also making friends I am convinced he will have for the rest of his life.

Dan has served as a youth pastor in several churches over the years. As I served beside him, I gained a wealth of knowledge as I watched teenagers try on different identities the way they tried on new clothes, discarding some in a matter of weeks, wearing others until they no longer fit. I will never forget the lesson I learned from Laura, a beautiful and talented girl who could have been anything in life that she chose to be. Instead, she had trouble finding work and rarely succeeded at any job she actually landed. I could not understand how such a beautiful girl could be so clueless about herself—until I met her parents.

It was painfully obvious that Laura's negative opinion of herself was firmly rooted in her parent's negative opinion of their daughter. Her room was a disaster because a clean room was important to her mother. Her grades were disgraceful because good grades were important to her father. She only dated guys who treated her like dirt because…well, she believed that she *was* dirt. Laura was graduating from high school, so I invited her to join me for a celebration lunch. When I asked what her plans were, she confided in me that all she really wanted to do was to graduate from high school, attend a local beauty school to become a hair stylist, and maybe one day open her own beauty shop. I was so excited for her because I could see her doing exactly that. On every youth trip, the girls flocked to Laura for help with their hair and makeup because she was so good at them! When I asked her what was keeping her from that dream, tears streamed down her face as she said, "My parents think that being a hair stylist is a ridiculous idea. If I choose to attend a beauty school instead of a four-year-college, I have to move out and do it all on my own." When I offered to talk to her parents, she shook her head and said, "It won't do any good." She was right. I did talk with them and nothing changed. But Laura did.

Laura graduated from high school and moved out of her home and in with a man who introduced her to drugs and alcohol. Years later I heard that she was living on the streets to support her habits. I have often wondered what would have happened if Laura's parents had chosen to support and encourage the gifts and abilities God had given their daughter instead of holding her hostage until she paid the ransom of bowing to their plan for her life.

In John 3:27 we find a simple but powerful truth, "God in heaven appoints each person's work" (NLT). God gives each person a special job to do. If you are doing what God wants you to do, your job is part of your ministry plan and you will be successful. God can and will work through you to do extraordinary things, no matter how ordinary your occupation may be in the eyes of man.

Over the years Dan and I have often talked with our children about a life plan. One of the things we always tell them is that if they want to be successful and contented in life, they need to discover what they love to do and then find a way to get paid doing it. Take a brutally honest inventory of your natural gifts, talents, and abilities, knowing that they are from God and are all part of your life plan. Ask those who know you best for their opinions and perspectives. Make a career choice based on persistent prayer and daily obedience to God. Discover what brings you the most satisfaction and do it. Life here is short. Do not waste it doing something you were not created to do. Choose your work carefully.

The Bible promises that God's plan is the best plan; the one for which we were created. Psalm 32:8 promises, "I will guide you along the best pathway for your life" (NLT). Not only does God agree to show us the plan, but He promises to provide all of the strength and resources needed to carry out that plan. His sufficient and constant power is unleashed by our choice to accept and follow His blueprint for victorious living.

We were created by the One who knows us best and loves us most. There are no accidents with God. He never has to say, "Oops!" Before we were ever conceived in the heart and mind of man we were conceived in the heart and mind of God. Wanted, loved, and planned since before the world began.

I know there are days when our life map seems completely wrong and impossible to understand, much less obey. Every emotion is shrouded in darkness and our hearts are numb, our steps paralyzed by fear and doubt. We are treading water in the storm-tossed sea of life, desperately longing to see Him walking on those treacherous waves toward us, rescue in His hand. It is in those shadowed moments that we must choose to trust the Plan Maker even though our faith is small. His ways are higher than our ways. His thoughts are higher than our thoughts, and one day, every one of our question marks will be yanked into exclamation points when we see that high plan as He sees it.

Today, my friend set aside your meager agenda. Lay down your incomplete life arrangement and look for God to meet you at the point of surrender—power and victory in His hands. Now *that's* a great plan.

Principle Two: Choose the Right Attitude About Work

She works with eager hands (Proverbs 31:13).

Working in an insurance office was one of my least favorite jobs. I soon discovered that I was evidently not alone in my lack of enthusiasm as I read the following note posted on the office bulletin board:

> If you don't believe
> In the resurrection of the dead
> You ought to be here
> Five minutes before quitting time!

Our attitude about our work will determine the success of our work. Scripture tells us that the Proverbs 31 woman literally "pounced upon" her work with "chosen delight." Notice the word "chosen." No job is perfect and no workplace is always wonderful, but we can learn to choose our inner attitude about our work regardless of the outer circumstances of our workplace. Like this woman, we can learn to train our heart and choose our attitude about our work.

The author of Ecclesiastes writes, "My heart took delight in all my work, and this was the reward for all my labor" (Ecclesiastes 2:10). In other words, joy in work can be found when we look for it. The Proverbs 31 woman chose an attitude that guaranteed success in her work. The right attitude in any workplace is to view our work as an act of worship to God. This woman's workplace was an altar upon which she laid her best efforts as an offering of praise.

The story is told of three men who were working on a large building project. "What are you doing?" one of the men was asked. "I am mixing mortar," he responded. The second man said, "I am helping put up this great stone wall." When the third man was asked, he replied, "I'm building a cathedral to the glory of God." We need to understand that what gives work eternal value and makes it successful is not the product or service we offer; it is doing the job faithfully to the glory of God. It doesn't matter if you close a million-dollar deal or do a million loads of laundry. If you do it unto God as part of your life worship of Him, you are a success.

The apostle Paul was a very successful man whose work ethic is made clear in Colossians 3:23: "Whatever you do, work at it with all your heart, as working for the Lord, not for men, since you know that you will receive an inheritance from the Lord as a reward. It is the Lord Christ you are serving." Every customer you serve or every child you hug, every toilet you clean or every deal you close can be an act of worship when it is done for the glory of God.

A survey by the Families and Work Institute found that 70 percent of people in the United States often dream about doing something different for a living. Books, consultants, and employment agencies offer to help us land our dream job. However, is finding a different occupation always the solution to job satisfaction or could the key to successful work be discovering a new approach to the work we already do? Twice in Colossians 3, Paul used the phrase "whatever you do" as a call for wholehearted service to the Lord. A wholehearted effort is difficult when working for a critical, ungrateful boss. Minimum effort then becomes a response that certainly seems justified under the circumstances. However, when our work is done for Christ and we view Him as our supervisor, we will strive to do our best all of the time. The boss may sign the paycheck, but the Savior issues our reward. Obviously, it's not wrong to seek work that fits our skills and interests, but it is pointless to move from one job to another without first settling the issue of who it is that we truly are serving in the workplace. Daily work takes on eternal significance when it is done for God.

Principle Three: Be Committed to Your Work

> She is like the merchant ships, bringing her food from afar
> (Proverbs 31:14).

The Proverbs 31 woman was deeply committed to her work as a wife, mother, and businesswoman. She went to the local market to purchase the necessities of life, but notice that she didn't stop there. She went shopping and bought unusual items from the ships of the merchants. In other words, she looked for ways to improve her work, refusing to be satisfied with mediocrity and unwilling to do only what was required of her.

We mistakenly assume that the less work we do, the less stress we will have. I have discovered, in my own life, that the better job I do, regardless of the job, the less stress I will have doing it. I believe we all have a built-in desire for excellence that naturally produces a commitment to excellence in everything we do, including work. However, that desire is often shrouded in the unrealistic expectations of others or lessened by the debilitating and negative evaluation of man.

Commitment will always produce the desire to do more than what is required. An ambitious young man asked the top salesman in his company for the secret of his success. "There is no great secret. You just have to jump at every opportunity that comes along," was his reply. The young man thought for a moment and then asked, "But how can I tell when an opportunity is coming?" The experienced salesman answered, "You can't. You just have to keep jumping."

Commitment in your work will be illustrated by the extra effort you are willing to give to your work. I once worked for a man who told me, "Mary, when you look at a plate of ham and eggs, you know that the chicken was involved. But the pig was committed." The psalmist writes, "Commit everything you do to the Lord. Trust him to help you do it and he will" (Psalm 37:5 TLB). Commitment is the first step in trusting God. A commitment to God influences every other commitment in life. David calls us to take delight in the Lord and to commit everything we have and do to Him. To commit everything to God means entrusting our life, family, job, and possessions to His control and guidance. To commit ourselves to God means to recognize and believe that He can care for us better than we can care for ourselves.

Principle Four: Set the Priorities of Your Work

> Commit your work to the LORD, and then your plans will
> succeed (Proverbs 16:3 NLT).

In order to be successful in the workplace, we have to find and keep a lifestyle of balance. Balance is the result of right priorities. The Proverbs 31 woman knew how to set and keep right priorities.

She was a planner. Proverbs 31:16 states that she "considers" a field. "Considers" means "determine or plan" and indicates forethought. In other words, she planned ahead, planning her work and working her plan. Every workplace is filled with people who have a plan for your life. If you don't set your life priorities, rest assured that someone else will set them for you. The priorities of our workplace should revolve around priorities that flow from a wholehearted commitment to God. The Proverbs 31 woman made that commitment, which is why her home and her life were under the control of God. Planning prevents chaos and keeps us focused on what is important. Have you noticed that the urgent things in life tend to barge in and demand attention while the truly important things in life wait to be chosen? We can spend an entire life on the urgent and completely miss the important—unless we plan.

She was disciplined. Proverbs 31:15 says that the Proverbs 31 woman "gets up while it is still dark." Discipline is the choice to do the right thing at the right time in the right way—even if it means working late into the night or getting up early in the morning. Where there is no discipline or control, there is failure and defeat. "A man without self-control is like a city broken into and left without walls" (Proverbs 25:28 RSV). Where there is no discipline, there can be no control or balance. Priorities in our work are hedges of safety put in place to prevent burnout, broken relationships, emotional bankruptcy, and physical exhaustion. Stress is the earmark of an undisciplined life.

Principle Five: Establish Goals in Your Work

> She considers a field and buys it; out of her earnings she plants a vineyard (Proverbs 31:16).

The Proverbs 31 woman obviously had certain goals in mind. After careful study and research, she found and bought a field. After working that field, she sold it for a profit and reinvested her earnings. You've probably heard the saying, "If you aim at nothing, you will hit it every time." Goals are important—for several reasons:

- Goals give direction.

- Goals motivate us.

- Goals stretch us.

- Goals are a measure of success.

- Goals create opportunities.

Many people miss wonderful opportunities because they are not looking for them or fail to recognize them when they come along. Opportunity is simply the result of hard work that is directed toward a goal. The word "opportunity" means "toward the port" and suggests a ship taking advantage of the wind and tide to arrive safely in the harbor.

Thomas Edison set a rather ambitious goal of coming up with a major new invention every six months and a minor invention every ten days. When he died, he had 1092 U.S. patents and more than 2000 foreign ones. J.C. Penney said: "Give me a stock clerk with a goal, and I'll show you a man who will make history. Show me a man without a goal, and I'll show you a stock clerk."

Goals are important, but it's just as important to realize that our goals will and must naturally change with the seasons of life. The response of many women, when confronted with the admirable example of the Proverbs 31 woman, is discouragement. Measuring up seems to be an impossible standard beyond human reach. Yet the Proverbs 31 woman is, in fact, our God-given example and the benchmark for which we must aim as women who seek God. Our only hope is a complete abandonment to the supernatural power of God at work in our lives—coupled with our intense obedience to Him. We also must realize that the portrait spans the entire lifetime of this woman and embraces different seasons of her life. Different seasons require different priorities and new goals in our work.

Principle Six: Don't Be Lazy in Your Work

> She sets about her work vigorously (Proverbs 31:17).
>
> She is energetic and strong, a hard worker (Proverbs 31:17 NLT).

I was raised to view laziness as unacceptable behavior. After my father died, my mother worked three jobs in order to support me, my brother, my sister, and our grandmother. I rarely saw my mother sit still as she tirelessly juggled the monumental demands on her time as a mother, pediatric nurse, babysitter, and housekeeper. As a result, no one in my life would ever call me lazy. As they say, "The fruit doesn't fall far from the tree." However, a busy life is not necessarily a productive life.

After 30 years in ministry, I have concluded that some people we label as "lazy" are actually dealing with an inner stress we fail to recognize. A lack of direction creates stress. The fear of disappointment and disappointing creates stress. A poor self-image creates stress. The condemnation and misunderstanding of others creates stress. The mountain of fear seems impossible to climb and the risk of failure too great. The result is a perception of laziness when, in reality, it is fear-driven paralysis laden with hopelessness and lack of motivation. The refusal to work or even to pursue excellence in work may be a cry for help.

Then, there are those who deliberately choose not to work at all or do only what is expected—nothing more. In fact, they go through life, hands stretched out in anticipation of others meeting their needs. These people are lazy! The dictionary is the only place where success comes before work. God is abundantly clear on His opinion of lazy people. The Proverbs 31 woman was not lazy. In fact, she was an extremely hard worker.

> The desires of lazy people will be their ruin, for their hands refuse to work (Proverbs 21:25 NLT).

> Lazy people are a pain to their employer. They are like smoke in the eyes or vinegar that sets the teeth on edge (Proverbs 10:26 NLT).

A lazy worker is an insult to God. If our work truly is an act of worship, laziness then becomes disobedience and a hindrance to worshipping God. Paul even goes so far as to say that we should avoid lazy people so we won't fall into the same trap: "Stay away from any Christian who lives in idleness and doesn't follow the tradition of hard work we gave you" (2 Thessalonians 3:6 NLT). In other words, there is absolutely no room in the life of a believer for laziness. If we refuse to work hard, we will never be successful in God's eyes. Most middle-class Americans tend to worship their work, work at their play, and play at their worship, a life philosophy that displeases God. He stands ready and waiting to not only equip and empower us to be the best employee we can be, but He also desires to pour out His blessings upon our work.

At the heart of our work should be the motive of love—love for the seeking heart, love for the wounded soul. God's greatest blessings come when we allow Him to use us in the workplace to share His message of love and restoration. Do not miss the fact that God strategically places us on a chosen mission field called a "job." A fellow employee needs to see a godly response to unfair criticism. A boss needs to witness the quiet, gracious spirit of submission—even in the face of a difficult job change. A fully devoted follower may be the only person who reaches out and ministers to a coworker in need. Make no mistake—everyone on the job is watching to see if we are the real deal. The way you live your life may be the most important sermon they ever hear. I challenge you to do your work unto Him and see what God does in and through a life committed to Him.

The Worker's Twenty-third Psalm

The Lord is my boss; I shall not want.
He gives me peace when chaos is all around me.
He reminds me to pray before I speak in anger.
He restores my sanity.

He guides my decisions that I might honor Him in all I do.
Even though I face absurd amounts of e-mail,
system failures, copier jams, back-ordered supplies,
unrealistic deadlines, staff shortages, budget cutbacks,
red tape, downsizing, gossiping coworkers, and whining customers,
I won't give up, for You are with me.

Your presence, peace, and power will see me through.
You raise me up, even when the boss fails to promote me.
You claim me as Your own,
even when the company threatens to let me go.
Your loyalty and love are better than a bonus check.
Your retirement plan beats any 401(k), and when it's all said and done,
I'll be working for you a whole lot longer!

AUTHOR UNKNOWN

Stress-Busters

From Ellen and Sally

Drink tea! God made wonderful teas to calm your mind and body. A cup of hot tea from the following list will help you settle down for a calming conversation with the Lord.

- Chamomile: relaxing anti-inflammatory

- Valerian: for high emotional stress

- Siberian (Eleuthero) Ginseng: supports entire body during everyday stress

God made beautiful flowers and leaves for aromatherapy: chamomile, cedar wood, sage, cypress, frankincense, geranium, jasmine, juniper, lavender, lemon, rose, and sandalwood. Enjoy their aromas as you sit quietly and pray.

○ ○ ○

- Get up 15 minutes earlier than usual so you can begin your day calmly instead of frantically.

- Take a 10-minute mini vacation. Sit back, close your eyes, and breathe deeply. Picture your favorite vacation spot and visit it for a few moments.

- Establish a set time during the day to return phone calls. That way, people can know when to expect your call.

- Have an impossible deadline? Ask if you can have an extension or if you can turn in the most important part of the project by the deadline and submit the rest later.

- Transition time is stress-reducing time. A friend suggests, "When I come home from work, I go straight to my room, close the door, lie down on my back, and close my eyes to relax my body and give my mind time to transition from work to home." Another friend washes her face before slipping into well-worn jeans and a comfy sweatshirt.

- Write out the recipes for five quick meals. Place the menu and ingredients in a plastic crate. When you are running late, just pull out the box and get started.

- Buy a small, inexpensive flower bouquet and set it on your desk. It will brighten your day.

- Listen to a daily devotional in the car on the way to and from work.

- Seven years ago I took up belly dancing for exercise. (No, I'm not kidding!) When I am really stressed, I pop in one of my CDs and dance with my veil. Since recommitting my life to Christ, I imagine myself giving my all to Him and dancing before Him in praise. It always helps to calm me down and refocus on what is important.

- Follow the principle that if your job is physical in nature, relax by doing something with your mind, such as reading. However, if your job is mental in nature, relax by doing something physical to relax.

- Bring a bag of fresh fruit and vegetables to snack on during the workday. Learn to take health breaks instead of coffee breaks.

- Bring a pair of comfortable shoes to work so you can walk during lunch.

- Practice deep breathing exercises you can do even when stuck in traffic or sitting at your desk.

- Keep a water bottle on your desk to drink from throughout the day.

- Take mini stretch breaks throughout the day. Do shoulder shrugs and neck stretches.

- Be assertive with people about your time. Though time is our most precious resource, most of us give it away too easily. That's poor stress management. When someone asks you for time, think about what you'll have to subtract from your current schedule. That will help you say no when you need to. "No" can be a great stress management tool. Angle your chair away from the door of your office to let others know you don't want to be disturbed.

- Post a list of steps your child needs to accomplish each morning. For young children, take photos of the child performing each task and tape it to the back of their door.

- Take the last 30 minutes of your day to list and prioritize tomorrow's tasks. Have your children pack their backpacks for the next morning and set them by the door.

- At the end of the day, take time to select your outfit for the next day. Include shoes, jewelry, purse, etc.

- Keep a list of phone numbers with you—your children's school, coaches, friends—so you can call if plans change unexpectedly.

- Keep one calendar with both work and family schedules. Have one copy with you and post one on the refrigerator.

- Get to the office 15 minutes early.

- Learn to delegate.

5

Expect Some Valleys

Yea, though I walk through the valley of the shadow of death...
PSALM 23:4 NKJV

Jehovah-Shammah: The Lord Is There

~ The Shepherd and His Sheep ~

The greenest grass is always found in the valley. Shepherds and sheep are well acquainted with the fact that both mountains and valleys are an inevitable part of life. Again, the shepherd is the one who has to figure out a way over the mountain and through the valley. If a sheep is injured, the shepherd must carry his sheep and tend to its wounds until they are healed and the sheep is ready to return to the fold. The shepherd's whole world revolves around the safety and comfort of his sheep, even in the deepest valley.

o o o

Valleys are a certainty of life. Your job is eliminated. You learn that your husband is having an affair or your teenage daughter is pregnant. Financial pressure suffocates dreams or the betrayal of a trusted friend inflicts a wound so deep and painful that you long for that valley of death. Each day is thick with fear and your heart is filled with disbelief. The valley may suddenly be before you in time of loneliness or in the shock of a dire medical diagnosis. No matter what valley may come, comfort and hope can be found in the message of the psalmist, "Yea, though I walk through the valley of the shadow of death, I will fear no evil" (Psalm 23:4 NKJV). Even though these words are most often shared at funerals or spoken at the bedside of someone who is dying, we must understand the truth that valleys filled with the dark shadows of death come to us all in many ways, but they always come courting stress.

The death of a loved one can derail a life. The death of a long-held hope can plunge us into a slimy pit of despair and darkness. Dreams that have slowly died or relationships that have abruptly ended can leave us stranded and alone in our own personal valley of death. While valleys may come in all shapes and sizes, one thing is certain—valleys will come. That being said, we must ask and answer the question, "How can we deal with the stress of a valley?"

God's Word provides a simple but significant four-step plan for shaping the right response to each and every valley we face: "Trust in the LORD with all your heart and lean not on your own understanding; in all your ways acknowledge him, and he will make your paths straight" (Proverbs 3:5-6).

Step One: We Must Respond with Faith

Trust in the LORD with all your heart (Proverbs 3:5).

It was advertised that the devil was putting his tools up for sale. When the day of the sale came, each tool was priced and laid out for public inspection. And what a collection it was. Hatred, envy, jealousy, deceit, pride, lying...the inventory was treacherous. Off to one side was a harmless-looking tool priced higher than all the rest, even though it was obviously more worn than any other tool the devil owned. "What's the name of this tool?" asked one of the customers. "That," the devil replied, "is discouragement." The customer asked, "But why have you priced it so high?" The devil smiled and explained, "Because discouragement is more useful to me than all the others. I can pry open and get inside a man's heart with that tool when I can't get near him with any other. It's badly worn because I use it on almost everyone, since so few people know it belongs to me."

Valleys are lined with disappointment and discouragement. Some people seem to thrive on adversity, emerging from their valley with greater strength and deeper faith. Others stumble and fall, giving in to discouragement and dropping out of the race. The difference in outcome is determined by the way we choose to handle discouragement.

We must respond to each valley with trust and faith. The word "trust" means "to lie helpless, face down" and is the picture of a servant waiting for his master's command or a soldier yielding himself to a conquering general. "Heart" refers to "the center of one's being." In other words, to trust God completely means that from the very center of our being, from the very core of our existence, we trust Him, totally abandoning ourselves in childlike faith to Him and His plan. We come, holding nothing in our hands, pushing no agenda, with one word in our heart—"whatever!" "Whatever You want me to do, Lord, I will do. Whatever You want me to say, Lord, I will say. Whatever You want me to think, Lord, I will think. Whatever path You have for me, Lord, I will walk."

If you are like me, you sometimes think you don't have enough faith. The amount of faith is not nearly as important as the right kind of faith—faith in God alone. A mustard seed is small but can still take root and grow—just like faith. Faith is also like a muscle. The more we use it, the stronger it becomes. We must remember that faith doesn't rest on what we have done, but on what Christ has done. As Paul says, times of stress accentuate the presence and power of God.

We can rejoice, too, when we run into problems and trials, for we know that they are good for us—they help us learn to endure. And endurance develops strength of character in us, and character strengthens our confident expectation of salvation. And this expectation will not disappoint us. For we know how dearly God loves us, because he has given us the Holy Spirit to fill our hearts with his love (Romans 5:3-5 NLT).

When the valleys come, we are tempted to abandon our faith and strike out in our own strength, when what we should do is embrace our faith in God, look for our Shepherd, and follow Him.

The story is told of a shepherd who tried to persuade his sheep to cross a swiftly flowing stream. Since sheep are naturally afraid of rapidly running water, the shepherd couldn't get them to cross. Then he had an idea. Picking up a lamb, he stepped with it into the river and carried it to the opposite shore. When the mother saw that the shepherd had safely led her lamb across the stream, she forgot her fear and stepped out in faith and into the rushing current. Soon, she was safely on the other side. The rest of the flock followed.

Faith rests in what Christ has already done on the cross and in our lives. Faith also hopes for what He will do for us in the future. Faith builds on the victories of yesterday to help us face the valleys of today and the questions about tomorrow. Faith in God is sure and certain, believing that God is who He says He is and that He will do what He says He will do. When we believe that God will fulfill His promises, even though we can't see a single promise materializing, we are exercising faith. Faith does not bypass pain. It does, however, empower us to deal with pain. Faith steps up to the bat and invites the opponent to throw his best pitch. Sometimes faith strengthens us, and other times, surprises us. Great faith is forged in the deepest valleys, beginning where our strength and power end.

I love the story of a missionary family, home on furlough and visiting friends. When it was time for dinner, the mother of the missionary children called her kids in. When her son burst through the door, she took one look at his hands and said, "Son, go wash those hands. They are dirty and covered in germs." With a scowl on his face, the little boy headed to the sink muttering, "Germs and Jesus! Germs and Jesus! That's all I hear about and I've never seen either one!" While we tend to say that seeing is believing, faith says that believing is seeing. Doubt creates mountains; faith moves them. Faith produces trust that shatters fear and controls stress.

Step Two: We Must Respond with Confidence

Lean not on your own understanding (Proverbs 3:5).

Stress feeds on human understanding. We sometimes try to handle life on our own, but our best human efforts can't come close to the power of God, our Shepherd. "Lean not" means "don't lean yourself upon." When the valley comes, we can respond with confidence in God instead of confidence in ourselves. This doesn't mean we should turn off our brain or ignore commonsense. God gave us those things to use for Him, but they are limited.

Admittedly, there are circumstances in life that make no sense—in human terms. Human understanding is impotent and loaded with stress. As Isaiah 55:9 says, "As the heavens are higher than the earth, so are my ways higher than your ways and my thoughts higher than your thoughts." When it comes to valleys, we must lean on God's understanding instead of our own.

Step Three: We Must Respond with Obedience

In all your ways acknowledge him (Proverbs 3:6).

We are to be walking, living illustrations of God. To "acknowledge" means "to show." In other words, we are to show God in everything we do. One of the most powerful evidences of a changed life is consistent obedience to God.

So brothers and sisters, since God has shown us great mercy, I beg you to offer your lives as a living sacrifice to him. Your offering

> must be only for God and pleasing to him, which is the
> spiritual way for you to worship. Do not change yourselves
> to be like the people of this world, but be changed within by
> a new way of thinking. Then you will be able to decide what
> God wants for you; you will know what is good and pleasing
> to him and what is perfect (Romans 12:1-2 NCV).

In this passage, the apostle Paul is not talking about a season of obedience, but rather a lifestyle of obedience. We can't obey every voice we hear. If we try, we will end up in total failure, carrying a heavy load we were never created to carry.

An old fable passed down for generations tells about an elderly man who was traveling with a boy and a donkey. As they walked through a village, the man was leading the donkey while the boy walked behind. The townspeople said that the old man was a fool for not riding the donkey. To please them, he climbed up on the animal's back and went on his way. When they came to the next village, the people said that the old man was cruel to let a child walk while he enjoyed the ride. To please them, the old man got off, placed the boy on the donkey's back, and continued on his way. When they reached the third village, people accused the child of being lazy because he was riding while the old man walked. The suggestion was made that they both ride. To please them, the man climbed on and off they went again. In the fourth village, the townspeople were indignant at the cruelty to the donkey because he was carrying two people on his back. The frustrated man was last seen carrying the donkey down the road.

Obedience to God is not a heavy load because we don't have to carry it alone. God's strength and power bear the burden of our obedience to Him. In Philippians 2:13 we find the promise: "God is working in you, giving you the desire to obey him and the power to do what pleases him" (NLT). God first works in us and then works through us to face every valley with a heart and life bent toward obedience to Him.

Dan and I had been married one year when we moved to Fort

Worth, Texas, so Dan could attend seminary. I desperately wanted a teaching job, but none was available. Instead, I was hired as a secretary in an insurance office. It was definitely not my idea of a dream job, but I had a plan. Every day, on my lunch hour, I called the school district's personnel office to ask, "Do you have a job for me yet?" After several weeks, a frustrated voice finally responded with the words I had been longing to hear. "Mary, will you teach anything anywhere?" Finally! I jumped at the job offer and made an appointment to visit my new classroom that afternoon. The principal escorted me up a flight of stairs, pointed to a door, and said, "That's your classroom. Good luck!" With a knowing smile, he turned and walked away...quickly.

Stepping into the classroom, I froze at the astonishing sight before me. Some children were jumping on desks while others crawled under tables, all screaming and yelling at the top of their lungs. Paper and food littered the floor. In the corner sat an obviously frazzled substitute teacher, who was desperately trying to gain control of her students...uh, make that *my* students. The classroom was in total chaos. My first thought was, *What have I gotten myself into?* The next few weeks certainly answered that question.

Each classroom was arranged in learning centers instead of desks. The students moved from center to center as they completed assignments, a plan that naturally invited noise. I learned that because of overcrowding, each teacher had been asked to select two children to form a new classroom...my classroom...and of course, each teacher had chosen his or her two most difficult students.

The first few weeks were a nightmarish battle for control. After losing my voice twice, my sister, Betty, a veteran first grade teacher, gave me some great advice. "The louder you are, the louder the children will be. If you want to get their attention, speak softly so they will have to be quiet in order to hear your voice." I put her advice into action the very next day. As the children entered the classroom, I greeted each one with a silent smile. In my hands was a brightly wrapped box. Curious, they asked, "What is that, Mrs.

Southerland?" I merely smiled and said nothing until every student was quietly seated. "I have a new plan," I began. "Sometime during the day, I will call your name once. If you hear my voice, you may choose one prize from our new prize box. If you don't hear my voice, you'll miss the opportunity to select a prize." It worked like a charm! In a matter of days, my students learned to listen for my voice above all others.

Even Jesus couldn't please everyone. Why do we think we can? Stress comes when we allow the many voices in life to drown out the only voice that really matters, the voice of God.

Step Four: We Must Respond with Trust

The only survivor of a shipwreck was washed up on a small, deserted island. He prayed fervently for God to rescue him. Every day he scanned the horizon for help, but none came. Exhausted, he eventually built a small hut out of driftwood as a shelter and a place to store his few remaining possessions.

One day, after scavenging for food, he arrived home to find his little hut in flames, the smoke billowing up to the sky. Everything was lost. Stunned with grief and anger, he cried, "God, how could You do this to me!" Early the next day, however, he was awakened by the sound of a ship approaching the island. It had come to rescue him. "How did you know I was here?" the weary man asked. "We saw your smoke signal," they replied.

God is always at work in our lives, even during our most stress-filled moments. When we entrust everything we are and everything we have to Him, when we depend upon His truth instead of our own understanding and choose to walk in obedience, He promises to "make [our] paths straight" (Proverbs 3:6). No matter how deep the valley, we can count on God for direction. In Proverbs 3:6, "make straight" means "to do right, to make smooth or to be evenly hammered." I love that truth! I can almost see my Father going before me, the hammer of truth in His hand, flattening every fear-filled obstacle, hammering down every mountain of doubt before me so that, when He has made a way, I can cross over. He straightens out crooked paths, improving my behavior and causing me to do the "right" things.

Valleys are best faced with a total abandonment to the Shepherd of the valley. How many times have we danced with joy on the mountaintop and then moaned and complained in the valley? God is Lord of the mountain *and* the valley. I suspect that the most powerful life is lived in the valley—not on the mountaintop. Every valley is surrounded by mountains and every valley has a Shepherd, a Shepherd who will walk with us through the valley, a Shepherd who will go before us, leading us out of the valley. When the psalmist wrote these words, he wrote my life message: "I waited patiently for the LORD; he turned to me and heard my cry. He lifted me out of the slimy pit, out of the mud and mire; he set my feet on a rock and gave me a firm place to stand" (Psalm 40:1-2).

No matter where you are today, your Father is there. No matter how deep or long the valley, He is with you, waiting for you to surrender all. Give Him your valley, knowing that He will surely lead you out. God has ordained that valley as an altar of sacrifice, an opportunity for Him to work through your broken heart and life. Keep your glance on the valley and your gaze on the Shepherd. Begin praising Him for your deliverance. It will surely come.

Stress-Busters

From Ellen and Sally

God-made foods were created to give you the fuel and nourishment you need. They also give you balanced energy useful for managing the positive and negative stresses you experience. The combination of a poor diet and living life according to your self-directed will is a formula for negative stresses which are known to lead to diseases such as cancer, diabetes, heart disorders, skin disorders, allergies, asthma, insomnia, and chronic fatigue syndrome. It's hard enough to figure out God's will when we refuse to align our will with His. Listen for God's guidance and follow Him.

Through prayer, search for God's plan for you. Dedicate yourself to eating God-made foods everyday. Eat stress-releasing immune-building foods while you are working hard at being productive.

Vegetables: acorn squash, beet greens (root), bell peppers (red and orange as well as green), broccoli, brussels sprouts, carrots, celery, chicory, Chinese cabbage, cilantro, citrus fruit, collards, dandelion greens, eggplant, fennel, garlic, green beans, jicama, kale, kohlrabi, mushrooms, mustard greens, onions, parsley, radishes, seaweed (kelp), spinach, sweet potatoes, turnip greens, watercress, zucchini

Fruit: apricots, avocadoes, bananas, blackberries, blueberries, kiwis, strawberries, tomatoes

Nuts and Seeds: almonds, pecans, walnuts, pumpkin seeds, sesame seeds

Whole-Grains: brown rice, oatmeal, quinoa

Dairy: yogurt (low to no sugar added)

Fish: cold water—mackerel, salmon, sardines, tuna

Legumes: soybeans, black beans, black-eyed peas

Poultry: turkey

Honey: raw and unfiltered

○ ○ ○

- Make four copies of the following thoughts. Post one on your refrigerator, tape one on your bathroom mirror, and keep one in your purse and one in your Bible. Refer to it often:

  In happy moments—praise God
  In difficult moments—seek God
  In quiet moments—worship God
  In painful moments—trust God
  In every moment—thank God
  And never underestimate the power of prayer!

- Take a deep breath in to the count of ten. Hold your breath for ten seconds and slowly exhale through your mouth for ten seconds. Repeat three times.

- Effective anger management is a tried-and-true stress reducer. Watch for the next time you find yourself becoming irritated or angry at something that really is trivial. Practice letting go, making a conscious choice not to become angry or upset.

- After a stressful situation is over, I create something that usually comes in the form of a painting project, decorating project, or sewing project. Reading fiction also helps me unwind.

- Being the spiritual giant that I am…my stress-buster is four Oreos eaten very, very slowly.

- Reject negative thoughts because negative thoughts breed stress. The promises of God "bust" anxieties and doubts, replacing them with peace-filled truths.

- Avoid watching distressing and/or violent programs on television. Your mind and emotions translate them as stressors.

- Gather and focus on the facts of a stress-filled situation. Stress feeds on the unknown.

6

Manage Your Fears

I will fear no evil; for you are with me; Your rod and Your staff, they comfort me.
PSALM 23:4 NKJV

Jehovah-Shalom: *The Lord Our Peace*

~ The Shepherd and His sheep ~

Sheep react without thought or reason, are easily frightened and upset, and require constant care and protection. When sheep scatter and run in confusion or fear, they tend to get themselves into situations they are unable to get out of on their own. Without the shepherd's help, the sheep would never survive. One of the greatest assets a shepherd has in these fearful circumstances is his voice. His sheep know his voice and will follow it, even through darkness and danger. As a result, the voice of the shepherd brings peace to his anxious sheep.

O O O

You could almost taste the fear lingering in the air over the valley of Elah. The monster had come, hurling vile promises and obscene threats as he strutted along the grassy slopes of the valley. He shook the ground with each thundering step, ready and eager to attack. Goliath, a nine-foot giant, the pride of Philistia, had arrived. A bronze coat of armor covered his massive frame as he taunted his prey with an iron-tipped spear and the contemptible promise of total destruction. A desperate group of Israelites, paralyzed with fear, had cowered in their tents for 40 days and nights, waiting for the end. Goliath had come, not only to taunt them, but to destroy them.

Then came day 41. As the sun inched its way over the mountains, I am certain neither Goliath nor the Israelites had any idea that this day would be different. A handsome teenager stepped into the valley of fear, fresh from the presence of God. David, the youngest in a family of eight boys, could not believe his eyes. In fact, he *refused* to believe his eyes. What he did believe was that his God was going to use him to take this monster down. I can almost envision the fear that must have surrounded David, but he stepped through his fear and into the power of God. Goliath not only met David that day, he met the Lord of heaven and earth—and the giant fell. Giants *always* fall in the presence of God. (See 1 Samuel 17.)

We face giants of some kind every day. Our first response is often anxiety and stress. It doesn't have to be. The psalmist writes, "I will fear no evil" (Psalm 23:4), a simple statement filled with a world of promise. Even in the midst of our personal valley laden with fear, we can rest assured that the battle belongs to God. Nothing, no evil, can harm us in any valley unless we choose to face that evil in our own strength. Instead, we can choose to rest in God and rely on His peace "that passes all understanding," (Philippians 4:7 RSV), knowing that whatever lies ahead is no surprise to Him. In fact, He has already been where we are going. That truth alone empowers us to face every tomorrow and walk through every valley with hope, knowing that whatever touches us passes through His hands with His permission.

It is not God's plan for us to dwell in fear or for fear to rule our lives. He has already set in motion the defeat and fall of every giant that we will ever face. Our responsibility is to step through our fear, confronting those giants in God's power while counting on the promise that God really is the same "yesterday and today and forever" (Hebrews 13:8). When we measure every tomorrow and every giant in life against the memory of Goliath's fall and David's trust in Almighty God, the Giant Killer, there is nothing we need to fear.

But sometimes we take our eyes off the Giant Killer and experience fear. And where there is fear, there is stress. Much of my stress comes from a personal failure to trust God. I demand His explanation for situations that make no sense to me. Like the pagan giant, I rant and rave because I can't hear His voice or understand His plan. I challenge Him to show Himself in the valley before me. It's a wonder that God has allowed me to live this long. I am so thankful for His love that looks beyond the ugliness of my doubting heart to the perfection of Jesus Christ. It is in that perfection where unshakable peace reigns, the same kind of peace we see in the life of Queen Esther.

Esther's parents died, leaving her orphaned as a child to be raised by a cousin named Mordecai. As a young teenage girl, Esther was placed in a circumstance I'm sure she would never have chosen for herself. Esther was selected to be a member of the king's harem, one of many girls from which the king could choose. I imagine the village girls were terrified when the king's men swept through the towns, searching for beautiful women who might catch the eye of the king. Frightened parents must have bribed those same men to overlook their daughters. Esther must have been just as frightened as every other girl, but still she was chosen. She left the only stability she had ever known to be thrust into a situation filled with fear and uncertainty. Talk about stress! The choices Esther made during one of the most frightening and stressful times of her life give us insight on how to manage our fears.

Choice One: Face Your Fear

> He [Mordecai]…asked Hathach to explain it to her [Esther] and to urge her to go to the king to beg for mercy and plead for her people (Esther 4:8 NLT).

> Then Esther told Hathach to tell Mordecai, "All the royal officers and people of the royal states know that no man or woman may go to the king in the inner courtyard without being called. There is only one law about this: Anyone who enters must be put to death unless the king holds out his gold scepter. Then that person may live. And I have not been called to go to the king for thirty days" (Esther 4:10-11 NCV).

Esther was open and honest in facing her fear. Our natural reaction, when confronted with fear, is to deny its existence by hiding it or pretending it is really something else, a habit that is both damaging and sinful.

The story is told of a little girl who developed the bad habit of lying. When her birthday came, she received a Saint Bernard but told all of her friends she'd been given a lion. When her mother heard this story, she was angry. "I told you not to lie. Honesty is very important. Now go upstairs and tell God you're sorry. Promise Him you'll never lie again." The little girl slowly climbed the stairs to her room, said her prayers, and then came back down to play. Her mother was waiting. "Did you tell God you're sorry?" she asked. "Yes, I did," her daughter quickly responded. "And God said that sometimes He finds it hard to tell a Saint Bernard from a lion too."

We must learn to face fear—in total honesty—instead of trying to bury it alive. I've discovered that when I bury live fears, they keep erupting all over my life, but when I face those fears and deal with them, I can bury them—dead—and they stay buried. Fear loves the darkness. Stress thrives in a heart filled with vain imaginings of what-if. When we choose to yank fear out of the darkness and into the light, it shrivels and dies.

Light brings every kind of goodness, right living, and truth
(Ephesians 5:9 NCV).

The LORD is my light and the one who saves me. I fear no
one. The LORD protects my life; I am afraid of no one (Psalm
27:1 NCV).

The Lord is our light. His presence always exposes fear and lets
us see it for what it really is—powerless. The only power fear can
have is the power we allow it to have. "God did not give us a spirit
that makes us afraid but a spirit of power and love and self-control"
(2 Timothy 1:7 NCV). God never intended His children to cower in
fear. Through Jesus Christ, God has furnished the strength, love,
and self-control that empower us to manage fear instead of allowing
it to manage us.

Where God's love is, there is no fear, because God's perfect
love drives out fear (1 John 4: 18 NCV).

In this verse, "perfect" means "complete." In other words, we are
incomplete without God's love. Fear flourishes in incomplete and
empty places because that void is home to stress and worry—until
perfect love shows up and sends that fear packing! The first choice
we must make when dealing with fear is to face it.

Choice Two: Share Your Fear

Esther sent this reply to Mordecai: "Go, gather together all
the Jews who are in Susa, and fast for me. Do not eat or drink
for three days, night or day. I and my maids will fast as you
do" (Esther 4:15).

We cannot face fear alone and expect to conquer it. Esther was
afraid. Yes, she chose to face her fear, but she did not choose to face
it alone. In fact, her first response was to reach out for help. To
whom did she turn for help and for comfort?

Family. "When we have the opportunity to help anyone, we should do it. But we should give special attention to those who are in the family of believers" (Galatians 6:10 NCV). While some of us can turn to an earthly family for support, many can't. However, as a child of God we can always turn to God's family when we are afraid.

Friends. "A person standing alone can be attacked and defeated, but two can stand back-to-back and conquer. Three are even better, for a triple-braided cord is not easily broken" (Ecclesiastes 4:12 NLT). The main work of friendship is to sustain each other and lighten the load. We were created to need others. The more you share your fear, the weaker it becomes.

God. "I prayed to the LORD, and he answered me, freeing me from all my fears (Psalm 34:4 NLT). Turn to God when you are afraid, knowing that while He allows fearful circumstances, He also monitors them and uses them for good in our lives. God understands your fear and He will deliver you.

Always in search of sweeter, greener grass, sheep tend to wander off into rocks and get into places from which they cannot escape. They will even jump down 10 or 12 feet, only to discover that they can't jump back up again. What do they do? Bleat like crazy. When the shepherd hears his sheep, he waits until the sheep is so weak from bleating that it can't stand. He then ties a rope around the exhausted sheep and pulls it to safety. When asked why he waits so long before rescuing the sheep, the shepherd replied, "I have to wait until the sheep has no energy left because sheep are so foolish that, in an attempt to escape, they would run over the edge of the rocks and be killed."

We are definitely sheep. We often try everything and everyone else before going to God as a last resort. When we reach the end of ourselves, choose to face fear head on, and are willing to trust God completely, He will surely save us.

Choice Three: Walk Through Your Fear

> I will go to the king, even though it is against the law, and if
> I die, I die (Esther 4:16 NCV).

Genuine courage is simply saying yes to God instead of backing down when we are afraid. Courage acts *with* fear, not *without* it. In Psalm 118:6, we find one of God's most precious promises to us as His children: "The LORD is with me; I will not be afraid. What can man do to me?"

Esther understood the situation perfectly. She knew that in order to win the battle over fear, she had to take action. She also knew that going to the king could very well mean her death. It was the law. To enter the king's presence without invitation meant a death sentence, but Esther chose to take charge of her fear and then to take control of her spirit and make it do what was right. Psalm 103:1-2 instructs us to do the same: "Praise the LORD, O my soul; all my inmost being, praise his holy name. Praise the LORD, O my soul, and forget not all his benefits."

In British Columbia, Canada, stood an old penitentiary. When it was being torn down, the workmen made an interesting discovery. The gates were made of steel and the windows were covered with iron bars, but the outer walls were made of wood, covered with clay and paper and painted to look as if the walls were thick metal. Anyone could have easily gone through the walls, but no one ever tried.

Getting a grip on fear always requires action on our part, even when we can't see what is ahead. It may be one tiny step or one puny choice. It may be a whispered prayer or a desperate cry for help, but God always honors the choice to walk straight ahead through fear.

Choice Four: Guard Against Fear

> These days of Purim should always be celebrated by the Jewish people, and their descendants should always remember to celebrate them, too (Esther 9:28 NCV).

> Esther's letter set up the rules for Purim, and they were writ-
> ten down in the records (Esther 9:32 NCV).

The Bedouin people, nomads of the desert, say that if a camel
is allowed to stick his nose inside a tent, he will quickly take it
over, destroying everything in his path. Fear is the same way. The
best way to guard against fear is to get ready and stay ready to deal
with it. We routinely live each day, barely keeping our balance on
a spiritual tightrope so that when disaster strikes, fear floods in and
we fall. God gives us several safeguards that will guard against fear
in our lives.

Remember the Victories

> Jesus Christ is the same yesterday and today and forever
> (Hebrews 13:8).

Why did Esther record what God had done and establish a celebration of God's victory? I believe one of the reasons was to plant
a hedge of protection for the future, a way to guard against fear.
Esther wanted to remember the power and faithfulness of God so
that when fear came again, she wouldn't stress out and give in to
defeat. I keep a "Victory Journal" for this very reason. In it I record
the spiritual markers in my life today that will remind me of God's
sufficiency tomorrow.

Get Rid of Sin

> Put away the sin that is in your hand; let no evil remain in
> your tent. Then you can lift up your face without shame, and
> you can stand strong without fear (Job 11:14-15 NCV).

Sin is an open invitation for fear, a formidable barrier to peace,
and a foothold for stress. Notice that this verse talks about a sin that
is in our hand. In other words, a cherished sin, a sin we really don't

want to give up. When we refuse to relinquish any sin, it becomes our master and we become its slave.

God is a jealous God who is serious about sin. "If I had cherished sin in my heart, the Lord would not have listened" (Psalm 66:18). When we put away our sin by turning from it and surrendering that sin to God, we can stand strong in God's power without shame or fear.

Over the years there have been many times when sin has hindered my relationship with God, but sin cannot ever dissolve that relationship. Nothing can separate us from His love (Romans 8:38 NLT). However, when we cherish and harbor sin, life inevitably spirals into a swirling cesspool of chaos where stress reigns supreme. A powerful promise is found in 1 John 1:9: "If we confess our sins, He is faithful and just to forgive us our sins and to cleanse us from all unrighteousness" (NKJV). Every time I read that verse, I am amazed by the hope it conveys. When we confess sin, God not only forgives that sin but removes the stain it leaves behind.

The stain of sin is one of Satan's favorite weapons in the war with stress. With it he births guilt and shame, hoping to cripple us spiritually. When we buy into his condemning lies, allowing them free reign, what we're really telling God is that sending His Son to die on the cross was not enough to cover our sin. I cannot even imagine what it must do to the heart of God as He watches us settle for so little when He offers so much. Knowing whose we are empowers us to live in peace with stress under His control.

Our first winter in North Carolina was interesting, to say the least. A fierce ice storm paralyzed Charlotte, the Queen City of the Carolinas. Many families were without heat for several weeks due to a massive number of power lines downed by ice-covered tree limbs that had broken under the unaccustomed weight of the ice. The greatest problems were in uptown Charlotte, an area known for its older but truly magnificent homes surrounded by gigantic oak trees. I had often driven those streets, amazed at the size and beauty of the oak trees lining driveways, their massive limbs sprawled across roofs and lawns. Each tree was almost perfectly shaped and, I would have thought, in perfect health. However, those same trees could not withstand the stress of the ice because of decay on the inside. What started as a tiny corruption at the center of the trees spread until each tree was so weakened that it was toppled by the winter ice storm. A cherished sin produces similar results in life. It corrupts from within, weakening a heart so that when a storm comes, the life is broken and powerless.

Train the Mind

> We fight with weapons that are different from those the world uses. Our weapons have power from God that can destroy the enemy's strong places...We capture every thought and make it give up and obey Christ (2 Corinthians 10:4-5 NCV).

The mind is the battlefield of life. In this verse, "take captive" is a military term, the picture of a guard standing watch. Someone had to assign that guard, indicating a choice. Left unguarded and untrained, the mind can become a toehold for the enemy. Fear trains us to anticipate the worst while faith teaches us to expect the best. "Faith means being sure of the things we hope for and knowing that something is real even if we do not see it" (Hebrews 11:1 NCV). We can train our minds to live in fear, or we can train our minds to live in faith. The most powerful way to train the mind is by filling it with Scripture. Jesus models this truth for us in His own life.

In Matthew 4 we read the account of Jesus being led into the wilderness for 40 days, where He was tempted three times by the devil. Each time, His weapon was the Word of God. He could have called all of heaven down to save Him. All of His Father's power was at His disposal, but all He needed was the Word of God. And that is all we need.

> I have hidden your word in my heart that I might not sin against you (Psalm 119:11).

> All Scripture is God-breathed and is useful for teaching, re-
> buking, correcting and training in righteousness, so that the
> man of God may be thoroughly equipped for every good
> work (2 Timothy 3:16-17).

It's important to remember that God's truth came before Satan's lies. When God's truth comes first, we will be able to recognize the lies of Satan and temptation will be easier to withstand. When we get away from God's Word, we become an easy target for both temptation and sin. Sin will either keep us from God's Word or God's Word will keep us from sin. In other words, when we deposit Scripture in our minds, God takes that Scripture and begins to reprogram thought patterns, teaching and thoroughly equipping us for life.

I have worn glasses for several years, but when I started speaking, they became a nuisance. They were either dirty or lost, or they constantly slid down my nose. Finally, I made an appointment with my eye doctor and went in for an exam. When I informed the doctor that I wanted to wear contacts, he seemed doubtful as he explained that my particular prescription would require me to wear a contact in my left eye for reading and a different strength contact in my right eye for distance. "Your brain is going to be very confused for several months," he warned. What else is new? I didn't see a problem—until I stepped off of a curb that wasn't there and reached for a glass that was closer than I thought, resulting in a sprained ankle and a water-soaked lap. Eventually, however, my brain did retrain itself and I could see perfectly. We can guard against fear by remembering the victories, getting rid of sin, and training our mind.

Pray Continually

> Pray at all times and on every occasion in the power of the
> Holy Spirit. Stay alert and be persistent in your prayers for
> all Christians everywhere (Ephesians 6:18 NLT).

In order to combat fear, we must be in a constant state of prayer about everything. If it's important to you, it's important to God. Paul tells us in 1 Thessalonians 5:17 to "pray continually." But many times, we pray only as a last resort.

I read about a kindergarten class that went to the local fire station for a tour. The fireman was explaining what to do in case of a fire. "First go to the door and feel the door to see if it's hot. If it is hot, fall to your knees! Does anyone know why you should fall to your knees?" A little voice spoke up. "Yeah, to start praying and asking God to get us out of this mess!" Exactly. The power to overcome fear comes from a praying heart, and the devil will do anything to keep us from praying. He laughs at our religious activities and mocks our human wisdom, but he trembles when we pray.

Be Alert

A bunch of recruits was taking a written examination. When one of them was asked why he wasn't working, he replied, "Sir, I have no paper or pencil." "Well," the instructor exclaimed, "what would you think of a soldier who went into battle with neither rifle nor ammunition?" The recruit thought for a moment, and then answered, "I'd think he was an officer, sir."

Unfortunately, too many Christians today think they are "officers" in God's army and don't really have to prepare for the battle. The warning of 1 Peter 5:8 is clear: "Be careful! Watch out for attacks from the Devil, your great enemy. He prowls around like a roaring lion, looking for some victim to devour" (NLT). One of the devil's favorite ways to "devour" us is with fear. Paul tells us, in Ephesians 6:18 to "stay alert" (NLT). "Alert" means "in all persistence." We need to be persistently watching for the traps of the enemy.

The ancient sport of falconry used trained hawks or falcons in the pursuit of wild game. When the "educated predator" was allowed to fly, however, it often rose too high for human eyes to see it. Consequently, a hunter often carried a small caged bird called a shrike. By watching the antics of the little bird, the man could always tell where his hawk was. How? The shrike instinctively feared the predator and cocked its head to keep it in view. I have often wished that God would provide a flashing red light and blaring siren to warn me of the devil's approach. Instead, He asks me to read and study the Bible, pray continually, and yield to the leading of the Holy Spirit in my life. With obedience comes sensitivity to the devil's schemes.

We need to keep our eyes open and be on guard against fear. We live in a world that stands against everything that we, as followers of Christ, stand for. If we aren't careful, we will fall behind or drop out of the race, a victim of fear and failure, which is exactly what Satan wants.

The King of Syria sent his whole army to capture the prophet Elisha. When Elisha's servant saw that they were surrounded on all sides, he was paralyzed with fear. Talk about a stressful situation! Elisha told him there was no reason to be afraid because "there are more on our side than on theirs" (2 Kings 6:16 NLT). The servant must have thought Elisha had lost his mind until Elisha prayed and the servant's eyes were opened. He then saw what no one else but Elisha could see. The mountain on which they stood was covered with horses and chariots of fire sent by God to protect the prophet. (See 2 Kings 6:8-23.)

How like us. Headed for heaven, we tremble at every earthly step, fearing that God's sure and eternal promises will break under our feet. Isaiah 12:2 promises: "God is the one who saves me; I will trust him and not be afraid. The Lord, the Lord gives me strength and makes me sing" (NCV). By resting completely upon God and taking His promises at face value, we can drive out fear and avoid the trap of stress. While fear leads to worry that strangles us, trust breaks the hold of fear in our lives. I know it seems impossible not to fear, but it must be because God never asks us to do anything He doesn't empower us to do. "Do not fear, for I am with you; do not be dismayed, for I am your God. I will strengthen you and help you; I will uphold you with my righteous right hand" (Isaiah 41:10).

Fear is a control issue that must be faced with a choice to trust.

The biblical antidote for fear always works: "I will trust, and not be afraid" (Isaiah 12:2). Choose to trust and you will not fear. Choose to fear and you will not trust. Isaiah 26:3 assures us, "You, Lord, give true peace to those who depend on you, because they trust you" (NCV). Trust involves giving Him first place and living as He wants us to live.

Playing God is the root of fear because when we play God, we are trusting in our own limited sufficiency. Be honest. Who is God in your life? Every opportunity to be afraid is also an opportunity to trust God. His presence should be enough to banish every fear found lurking in the shadowed corners of our hearts and minds. "I will fear no evil, for you are with me," the psalmist proclaims in Psalm 23:4. The verse goes on to promise, "Your rod and your staff, they comfort me." The rod and staff are opposite ends of the same stick. The rod is the blunt end used by the shepherd to fight off attackers of his sheep. The staff is the crooked end, used by the shepherd to pull sheep out of tough places. Let me be perfectly honest. Sheep are stupid. The shepherd must constantly rescue them from some crevice where they have fallen because they have wandered outside his care. We have nothing to fear, not because we are clever or self-sufficient, but because we are God's sheep. Now is the time to take our fears and lay them at the feet of our Shepherd, the One who holds the rod and staff in His hand. Through Him, we can learn to manage fear and stress instead of allowing fear and stress to manage us.

Stress-Busters

From Ellen and Sally

God has provided you with physical tools to combat fear. In fact, the body's response to fear involves the release of hormones that prepare you for "fight or flight." A problem with today's society is they do neither. Instead, fear is internalized and the negative energy is leashed onto one or more organs. Exercise is the accepted but often ignored answer to stress caused by fear.

○ ○ ○

- My stress-busters include a warm kitty snoozing on my lap while I read or watch TV, making lists and crossing things off, and eliminating unnecessary activity from my life.

- Visit a pet store and play with a kitten or puppy.

- Blow bubbles or create something with Play-Doh.

- Buy packing bubble wrap and pop all of the bubbles.

- Buy a brand-new box of crayons and a coloring book and then just color. Don't worry about staying in the lines.

- I work out three times a week and spend a good bit of time in stillness.

- Turn off the phone for an hour. Use that time to leave your fears to God.

- Recall and revisit favorite memories.

- Start a "Joy Journal" in which you record daily blessings. Read it at least once a week.

- Hang pleasant-sounding chimes in your backyard. When stress threatens, take a ten-minute break. Pour yourself a glass of iced tea, sit in the porch swing or rocker...listen to the chimes... breathe deeply...watch the birds...remember that God really is in control.

- In my twenties I loved stress as if it was something to be proud of. In my thirties I went shopping, ate chocolate, read God's Word and prayed a lot, but continued the stressful lifestyle. In my forties I have hated stress and taken steps to manage it more effectively. I've eliminated needless jobs I once did. I'm more organized in order to prevent any unnecessary stress. I've stopped talking on the phone unless it's important. I try to balance my emotions more than I did when I was younger because I see how out of control they can get. The "dead to self principle" has played a big role in that one. Reading the Bible and praying are more important than ever in my life, knowing that He is my only hope to stay out of the stress trap. I thought I had power to control stress when I was younger, but now know that I don't. Stress brings me to a humble state of mind daily. That humble state (whipped to a pulp) actually is my escape from the stress trap.

7

Celebrate the Battle

You prepare a table in the presence of my enemies; You anoint my head with oil; my cup runs over.
PSALM 27:5 NKJV

Jehovah-Nissi: *The Lord Our Banner*

~ The Shepherd and His Sheep ~

Looking after sheep has never been an easy task, and was especially difficult in biblical times. Herds were often quite large, containing thousands of sheep. The flocks spent a good part of the year in the open country. Watching over them required a great deal of attention. The shepherd typically carried certain equipment necessary to care for his sheep:

- A goatskin bag in which food or other items were carried
- A sling for defending himself and the flock against wild animals
- A cloak that was also used for nighttime bedding
- A stick (rod) about a yard long with a knob on one end, used to fight off enemies of the sheep

- A shepherd's crook (staff) that looked somewhat like a modern cane used to pull sheep out of tight places

The shepherd also carried a flute, a fact I find interesting. I believe the shepherd used the flute for his own entertainment as well as to calm his flock, but I can also see him playing the flute in praise, thanksgiving, and joy to God, the Good Shepherd.

○ ○ ○

Many life battles are lost because our confidence and faith in God are eroded under the persistent battering of daily stressful situations. We often fail to recognize and embrace the truth that God defines and refines us in the midst of battle. If the battle truly belongs to God, we win! We win before the first shot is fired. We win before one step of the battle plan is taken.

I would naturally assume that a victory banquet would be held *after* the victory was won. However, the Hebrew people blew that idea right out of the water when they held victory banquets *before* the battle even began. If I had been there, I would have surmised that the Hebrews were either ridiculously arrogant or people of great faith. The truth is that there was an anointing on their lives, a sign of being chosen by God. And because they were a chosen people, their faith grew strong and freed them to stand on the undeniable truth that they could count on their God. Celebrating the battle's outcome was simply a matter of celebrating God, acknowledging His power on their lives, and walking by faith in the victory provided before the battle was even fought.

We, too, are a chosen people, created by the hand of God. We can sit down at the table of victory every moment of every day because no matter what happens, if God is for us—we win! The battle really is for our good.

Honestly, I must admit I'm not always a big admirer of God's plan for refinement by fiery trials and unwanted wars. However, I am so thankful that He is more committed to my character than to my comfort, disregarding my pitiful complaints and frequent whining. The greatest and most valuable growth comes by way of the fiercest battle. How many times in life do we fight against God-ordained wars and battles? I tend to look for the nearest escape route when the first shot is fired. And is it just me, or is there always a battle ahead? Are we willing to step out in faith, celebrating the already won battle at the victory table set before us?

I really believe our faith is measured by how we handle each battle that comes our way. It may be a skirmish to carry out God's holy vision, a war against those who seek to undermine God's calling, or the age-old conflict of good versus evil. The battlefield is not nearly as important as our choice to align ourselves with God's plan and step out in faith of the battle already won—which brings us to the powerful stress-buster of praise.

Many Christians neglect praise entirely because they are afraid of it, shoving it out to the edge of their spiritual journey, fearful that it might make them uncomfortable. Others base their entire faith on praise while they neglect the Word of God, leaving the service to someone else because they are busy praising God. Both viewpoints are wrong, out of balance, and generate stress. The truth is that heartfelt, genuine, God-honoring, stress-busting praise and thanksgiving are acts of spiritual obedience and should be practiced by every believer. We can learn to practice praise, and in doing so, deal with stress in a powerful way.

We Must Understand What True Praise Is

Praise is not optional for a fully devoted follower of God. Praise is essential to a vital faith, is a command of God, and a fundamental stress-buster. I believe the problem lies in understanding what true praise really is.

> Praise the LORD. Praise God in his sanctuary; praise him in his mighty heavens. Praise him for his acts of power; praise him for his surpassing greatness. Praise him with the sounding

of the trumpet, praise him with the harp and lyre, praise him
with tambourine and dancing, praise him with the strings
and flute, praise him with the clash of cymbals, praise him
with resounding cymbals. Let everything that has breath
praise the LORD. Praise the LORD (Psalm 150:1-6).

In Psalm 150, the psalmist offers a beautiful and detailed picture
of true praise. Praise is more than spoken words, singing songs, and
lifting up hands in worship. True praise is the celebration of God's
power, His works, His greatness, and His control. Praise is the natural by-product of a heart that is fully committed to God as well as
the treasure of a life completely surrendered to Jesus Christ.

Praising God motivates us to know more about Him; the more
we know about God, the more we will praise Him. Praise should
be as natural as breathing, the authentic and innate expression and
ongoing celebration of a love relationship between God and man.
The psalmist says it well, "Because your love is better than life, my
lips will glorify you. I will praise you as long as I live, and in your
name I will lift up my hands" (Psalm 63:3-4).

I believe that, in God's eyes, an obedient life is the highest offering of praise we can offer. At the heart of praise is an attitude of
acceptance that ultimately and naturally demonstrates faith. Faith
is the root from which praise grows. In turn, praise strengthens our
faith and demolishes stress. Stress simply cannot abide in a heart
that is filled with praise.

We Must Recognize the Power of Praise

Man set aside one day a year to be thankful. God set aside a
lifetime. Yet I find few Christians whose lives are continually filled
with thanksgiving and praise. I think I know why. We do not understand the true meaning of praise and grossly underestimate the
power that praise holds. Praise can alter life's parameters to include
trust and acceptance in the face of any crisis. The power of praise

can make each ordinary moment of every ordinary day a season of true celebration and new meaning. Praise not only pleases God, it changes our life perspective, filling each moment with faithful trust and fresh joy.

Praise Pleases God

> Give thanks in all circumstances, for this is God's will for you in Christ Jesus (1 Thessalonians 5:18).

Most of us are not very good at maintaining an attitude of praise and thanksgiving. We're like the little boy who, on his return from a birthday party, was asked by his mother, "Bobby, did you thank the lady for the party?" The boy thought for a moment before saying, "Well, I was going to, but a girl ahead of me said, 'Thank you,' and the lady told her not to mention it. So I didn't."

I must admit that the thought of bringing pleasure to God tilts my world just a bit. Nevertheless, we belong to Him, and just as we are pleased when our children obey us, God is pleased when we obey Him. Obedience to God is not complicated. It's simply determining and doing His will. An obedient life is praise in action and brings God pleasure. God seeks people who long to truly worship and praise Him. John tells us that when we do His will, God is pleased. "If you love me, you will obey what I command" (John 14:15). What an amazing thought, that I can bring God pleasure with my praise.

Praise Deepens Trust and Joy

> He who sacrifices thank offerings honors me, and he prepares the way so that I may show him the salvation of God (Psalm 50:23).

Chuck Swindoll says, "The sovereignty of God is the Christian's security blanket." Praise turns trials into faith-builders as we learn to measure our problems against God's limitless power, transforming the stumbling blocks of today into stepping stones for tomorrow.

At the heart of praise is a childlike trust and acceptance of God's control over circumstances. Honestly, there are times when I can neither explain nor understand those circumstances, but I can go through them, knowing that God is at the helm of my little boat. My husband grew up driving the family ski boat, pulling family members and friends across a lake as they learned to water-ski. Consequently, he is an excellent boat driver, especially for children or any novice on skis. Both Jered and Danna learned to ski behind a boat driven by their dad. I knew they preferred Dan to other drivers, but I didn't realize just how important it was to them until someone else tried to take the wheel.

Several years ago, we invited some friends to join us for a few days at the lake. We met Josh and Sarah at church and had become good friends. Our kids seemed to enjoy theirs. It was perfect. Well, almost. After several days of nonstop skiing, Dan was exhausted and asked the kids for a breather. "Guys, let me have one day off and then I'll be set for the rest of the week," he pleaded. Josh immediately volunteered to drive the boat, assuring Dan and the kids that he was an expert. Doubt spread across the faces of our kids, but since Josh was their only option, they grabbed their life jackets and skis and headed for the boat. Dan grabbed a snack, a cool drink, and the novel he had been trying to read for weeks and headed for the nearest hammock, a gloriously unplanned day to call his own.

Actually, it turned out to be a gloriously unplanned *hour* before we heard our boat returning to the dock. Jered and Danna climbed out of the boat and headed straight for their dad. "Josh has no idea what he is doing, Dad" Jered quietly but firmly explained. "He almost killed me!" Danna reported with her usual drama. Jered summed up a 30-minute play-by-play account of the disastrous afternoon by announcing, "Dad, I'll ski when you're driving the boat!"

Praise frees us from having to understand our circumstances, knowing that God is in control. A heart filled with praise does not have to understand every detail of the circumstance. In fact, the details really don't matter. What *does* matter is that God is aware of every minute detail, monitors the circumstance, and shapes it to fit His plan.

Praise Transforms Tragedy into Triumph

> These [trials] have come so that your faith—of greater worth than gold, which perishes even though refined by fire—may be proved genuine and may result in praise, glory and honor when Jesus Christ is revealed (1 Peter 1:7).

Fanny Crosby was six weeks old when she lost her vision because of a doctor's error in applying the wrong medicine to her eyes, a mistake that determined the course of her life. She could have easily become bitter, but instead she chose to praise God. I'm certain she did not understand all of the reasons for her lot in life, but I'm equally certain she made the choice to build a monument of praise on that lot instead of resurrecting a tombstone of bitterness. Fanny Crosby chose to praise God by writing more than 8000 hymns of praise, including "All the Way My Savior Leads Me," "Blessed Assurance," and "To God Be the Glory." Praise made the difference between tragedy and triumph.

Praise Invites God to Work

> Sing to God, sing praises to His name. Prepare the way for him who rides through the deserts (Psalm 68:4 NCV).

> But You are holy, enthroned in the praises of Israel (Psalm 22:3 NKJV).

Praise is the conduit of power in our lives, inviting God to work. When we honestly express our feelings to Him and then choose to give thanks, healing begins. In fact, praise provides a highway upon which the Father brings deliverance and blessing. Stress and anxiety fade as peace floods the heart filled with praise. Don't miss the life-changing truth that we can enthrone God in every situation of our lives by praising Him. In fact, praise transforms everyday surroundings into a dwelling place for God. It's from that throne of praise that He dispenses healing and deliverance. Praise tunes us into His sovereignty and allows us to experience the reality and power of His presence.

Praise Strengthens Our Prayer Life

> I will praise You, for You have answered me, and have become my salvation (Psalm 118:21 NKJV).

Prayer is not only a remarkable privilege and spiritual responsibility, it is worship. There is the prayer of petition when we seek forgiveness, lay needs before God, and intercede on behalf of others. Then there is the prayer of thanksgiving when we offer praise to God for who He is and for what He has done.

We sometimes make prayer so complicated when it is really so simple. Prayer is conversation with God. I love the story of a grandfather who, when walking past his little granddaughter's room one night, saw her kneeling beside her bed with her head bowed, eyes closed, and hands folded. As he listened, he was surprised to hear the little girl repeating the alphabet. "What are you doing?" he asked. With a smile, she explained, "I'm saying my prayers, but I couldn't think of just what I wanted to say. So I'm just saying all the letters so God can put them together however He thinks best." The words we say when we pray are not nearly as important as the attitude of the heart behind the prayer, and when that attitude is praise, the prayer is powerful.

Praise Devastates Satan and His Forces

> We will shout for joy when you are victorious and will lift up our banners in the name of our God (Psalm 20:5).

Victory and praise go hand in hand. Satan knows that. Through continual prayer, through the power of God's Word, and through faithful praise we declare our trust in God to deliver us. Praise lifts up the shield of faith in spiritual warfare. Praise makes a frontal attack on doubt and fear. Even in the midst of Satan's best efforts, we can find victory when we praise Him.

We Must Choose to Practice Praise

A heart that chooses to praise God demonstrates what God can do in a life. Have you noticed how much of the Christian life is wrapped up in the word "choice"? Just as we can choose our inner attitude, no matter what our outer circumstances may be, we can choose to cultivate the habit of praise. If we wait until we *feel* like praising God, we may never praise Him. Praise has nothing to do with feelings and everything to do with facts. And the facts are extraordinary.

- We are loved, wanted, and planned by God.
- We were created in response to God's unique plan.
- God sent His only Son, Jesus Christ, to pay for our sins—every single one of them.
- We can have a personal relationship with Jesus Christ.
- Through that personal relationship with Jesus, we have access to all that God is and all that God has.
- God will never leave us or forsake us.
- God meets our every need.
- Jesus will return one day to take us home to heaven, where we will spend eternity with Him.

My friend Melissa is the consummate hostess. She makes entertaining look so easy. To her, a dinner party for 50 guests is a simple feat. Just shoot me now! One of her favorite preparations is the dinner table. When I'm expecting company, the first guest to arrive has the honor of setting the table with whatever she can find in the way of tablecloths, silverware, glasses, and…you get the idea. Not

Melissa. I've seen her table completely and beautifully arranged days before the anticipated dinner party or holiday meal. When I asked her why she went to such elaborate lengths, her answer made me stop and think. "I love having the table set early because every time I walk past it, I think of the people who will sit in those chairs and pray for them. I think of their favorite dishes and look forward to preparing each one. I guess you could say that I enjoy the party long before it begins." That's the idea behind praise. We can praise God for what He will do long before He does it. We can prepare a victory table before the battle begins, knowing that the battle belongs to our God. And don't you know that a prebattle victory party irritates the fire out of the enemy? I love that.

It's said that in Africa a tree produces the "taste berry," a unique fruit that literally alters taste buds so that everything that's eaten after eating the berry tastes good and sweet. Praise is the "taste berry" of the Christian's life. When our hearts are filled with praise, when we choose to praise God, no matter what, stress fades into the background of a battle won before it begins, life is sweet, and all is good. Party on, my friend.

Stress-Busters

From Ellen and Sally

Stress causes both positive and negative physical reactions. A well-nourished body has a strong immune system, a well-oiled nervous system, a steady circulatory system, and so much more that will provide you with the energy needed to manage stress. Whatever you put into your mouth, swallow, and digest causes something to change in your body. What you choose to eat during and after stress will make a difference. Manage and celebrate your battles with better food choices.

When you find yourself in overload, you can jump-start your physical and mental health by cleansing your body with a detox program, a process of removing toxins from your body. On a daily basis, drinking glasses of water with lemon is helpful. Dark green foods such as spinach, broccoli, parsley, chlorella, and spirulina help keep your systems clean, as do leafy vegetables. Try the good-tasting green drinks. Pineapple, garlic, and olive and fish oils are cleansing foods. At the least, stay away from sugar, fruit juices, bad fats, dairy, and wheat products. No sodas or coffee. Drink green, red, white, and peppermint teas instead. Supplements such as B-complex, alpha lipoic acid, and milk thistle are helpful. Fasting for one to three days under the guidance of a health professional is a life-renewing experience.

○ ○ ○

- My number one stress-buster is having a grateful heart. Find something you're truly grateful for and praise God for it. Praise Him for His plan and take comfort in that the stress you are facing may be bigger than you, but not bigger than your God.

- Pray the psalms.

- If an unpleasant task faces you, do it early in the day and get it over with.

- Plan something rewarding for the end of your stressful day, even if it is only a relaxing bath or half an hour with a good book. Don't spend this time planning tomorrow's schedule or doing chores you didn't get around to during the day. Remember that you need time to recharge and energize yourself. You'll be much better prepared for the stress of tomorrow.

- Laugh...a lot. Enjoy these humorous stories shared by friends:

On Palm Sunday, my five-year-old niece, Stephanie, sat on my lap while listening to the pastor describe Jesus' approach to Jerusalem and how the crowds cried, "Hosanna, Hosanna!" At that, Stephanie perked up and began to sing, "Oh, Hosanna, now don't you cry for me!"

During a visit to Grandma and Grandpa's, our two young daughters watched from the breakfast table as a man came to the back door. When the visitor left, Grandpa explained that he was an appraiser. "What's an appraiser?" the younger child asked. Before Grandpa had a chance to explain, older sister quickly cleared up the matter. "He's a Praiser. He goes to church every Sunday."

One Sunday in church, members were praising the Lord for what He had done in their lives that week. Mr. Segault said the roof of his house had caught on fire, but fortunately, a neighbor had seen it, and the possible disaster was averted with only minor damage. A minute later, a woman stood up. "I have a praise too," she said. "I'm Mr. Segault's insurance agent."

My husband and I are raising four of our eight grandchildren, ranging in age from nine to thirteen. School mornings often find me stressed by 6:10 when I head outside to watch for the school bus. We live on a hill, so I can see the bus as it nears our home. Living in the country, away from city lights blesses us with tons of stars at that early morning hour. I often use that waiting time to pray, asking God to forgive and calm my stress-filled heart. I then soak up the quiet and peace. The glory of God's creation really puts my kid problems in perspective. I can then turn my cries of repentance into praise and worship. Nothing like seeing how big my God is to make everything else fall into place.

8

Count on Grace

Surely goodness and mercy shall follow me all the days of my life.
PSALM 23:6 NKJV

El Elyon: *The Most High God*

~ The Shepherd and His Sheep ~

The shepherds of Palestine wore a loose, heavy coat that was gathered about the waist with a cord. On cold nights, the shepherd wrapped the coat around himself for warmth. In the loose folds of this coat, he carried little lambs that were too young and too feeble to follow the flock. When the Eastern shepherd brings his sheep back to the fold each night, he stands at the door, counting each one and placing his hand on the head of each animal as it enters the fold. The shepherd is diligent in this daily practice of touching his sheep. Why? If the sheep didn't feel the daily touch of his shepherd, it would soon fail to respond to the voice of the shepherd, a reality that would spell disaster. The sheep wouldn't hear the warning shout of the shepherd when danger loomed. Sheep are at the mercy of their shepherd.

○ ○ ○

Because God created us, He has the right of ownership in our lives, but because He's a God of grace, He gives us a choice, a free will, and the option to walk away. And we do. "We all, like sheep, have gone astray, each of us has turned to his own way" (Isaiah 53:6). We walk away from His heart of unconditional love straight into the arms of sin-filled stress. But instead of condemning us, God chose to send His own Son to pursue us, to find and redeem us at the highest possible cost, His Son's life. That is grace, my friend, and it chases us, goodness and mercy in hand, every moment of every single day that we live.

I love the story of the shepherd who notched the ear of a lamb born to his flock. The lamb rightfully belonged to the shepherd but wandered away from the fold. For months, the shepherd searched for the lamb without success. While attending an animal auction, the shepherd spotted a lamb bearing his mark on its ear. Rushing to the auctioneer, the shepherd explained, "I can see my mark on that sheep. It's mine." The auctioneer responded, "You have to bid on the sheep and pay for it like everyone else." Undeterred, the shepherd bid and paid an exorbitant price, far higher than any reasonable market value. It didn't matter. The lamb belonged to him twice over—once because he owned the sheep from birth and once because he redeemed the sheep from the auction block.

God has a right to own us because He created us and because He has paid for us with the blood of His own Son—an outrageous price far above our market value—in order to redeem us back again. Just as sheep need constant care and watching, our Shepherd is forever with us. Just as sheep are easily spooked and panic, we often run when confronted with a problem or dilemma. Just as sheep will hear their shepherd's voice and come back to him, we hear our Shepherd's voice and return to His persistent love. When we are wounded, unable to come to the Shepherd, the Shepherd comes to us and carries us in the safety of His arms. We often find ourselves in places from which we can't easily escape, so the Shepherd finds us and saves us from ourselves.

Just as sheep take for granted the care and concern of their shepherd, we take for granted all that Christ is and all that He has in store for us. The Shepherd feeds and waters us through His Word. Even while we are busy or asleep, the Shepherd is forever standing watch over us, waiting and listening for our voice when we cry out to Him. When the enemy comes as a roaring lion to devour us, our Shepherd positions Himself between us and destruction, laying down His life for His sheep. That's grace.

As God's children, we will not only be marked by His joy but inevitably will be painfully marked by suffering and difficulty as well. When we begin to see those difficult circumstances as precious notches of His love, evidence of His healing power and transformation, stress is consumed by trust. It must be painful for Jesus Christ to watch those marks being burned, pierced, and notched into our lives because He loves us. The thought of anyone hurting one of my children elicits fierce emotions and long claws. Jesus is our Shepherd and we are children of God's grace.

I can still see my fifth grade Sunday school teacher, Mrs. Cash, as she wrote the word "grace" on the classroom chalkboard. "What does the word 'grace' mean to you?" she quietly asked. Even though the word was somewhat familiar, I had no clue what grace actually meant. Mrs. Cash simply smiled at my best friend, Katrina, who raised her hand to explain that "grace" was a girl's name. Hmm... evidently, that wasn't the correct answer. The pastor of the small country church I attended often used the word "grace" in his sermons, and many of the songs we sang at church contained the word "grace" in their lyrics. Yes, I'd heard about grace and sung about grace, but when it came right down to it, grace was ambiguous to me at best. I'm afraid that's the case with many of us today. If we are not personally experiencing, walking in, and serving through the grace of God, we are missing God's best. Mrs. Cash simply turned again to the chalkboard and wrote this acronym that is now inscribed in my Bible and in my heart:

G God's

R Riches

A At

C Christ's

E Expense

All that God is—all that God has—is available to us now and forever. With every breath we take and every beat of our heart, His riches are ours because of what Jesus Christ did on the cross. Those infinite riches are credited to our life account, deposited there by the Son of God. His supply of grace is infinite. The work of grace is miraculous and is unleashed the moment we fully surrender to God.

> Surely goodness and mercy shall follow me all the days of my life (Psalm 23:6).

The true story is told of a little girl who went to her bedroom closet and pulled a glass jelly jar from its hiding place. Tess poured out all the change and carefully counted it three times, just to be sure. The total had to be exactly right. Carefully placing the coins back in the jar and replacing the cap, she slipped out the back door and walked the six blocks to the local drugstore with the big Red Indian Chief sign above the door.

The little girl walked in, heading for the pharmacy. She waited patiently for the pharmacist to notice her, but he was too busy talking with another man. Tess twisted her feet to make a scuffing noise. Nothing. She cleared her throat with the most disgusting sound she could muster. No good. Finally, she took a quarter from her jar and banged it on the glass counter. That did it!

"And what do you want?" the pharmacist asked, clearly irritated at the interruption. "I'm talking to my brother from Chicago, whom I haven't seen in ages." "Well, I want to talk to you about my brother," Tess answered back in the same annoyed tone. "He's really, really sick…and I want to buy a miracle." "I beg your pardon?" asked the pharmacist. "His name is Andrew, and he has something bad growing inside his head. My daddy says only a miracle can save him now. So how much does a miracle cost?"

"We don't sell miracles here, little girl. I'm sorry, but I can't help you," replied the pharmacist in a slightly softer voice. "Listen, I have the money to pay for it. If it isn't enough, I'll get the rest. Just tell me how much it costs," she pleaded. The pharmacist's brother, a well-dressed man, stooped down and asked the little girl, "What kind of a miracle does your brother need?" "I don't know," Tess replied as her eyes filled with tears. "I just know he's really sick and Mommy says he needs an operation. But my daddy can't pay for it, so I want to use my money." "How much money do you have?" asked the man from Chicago. "One dollar and eleven cents," Tess whispered. "And it's all the money I have, but I can get some more if I need to." The man smiled and said, "Well, what a coincidence. One dollar and eleven cents is the exact price of a miracle for little brothers. Take me to where you live. I want to see your brother and meet your parents. Let's see if I have the kind of miracle you need."

That man was Dr. Carlton Armstrong, a surgeon specializing in neurosurgery. The operation was completed without charge, and it wasn't long until Andrew was home again and doing well. Mom and Dad were happily talking about the chain of events that had led them to this place. The mother said, "That surgery was a real miracle. I wonder how much it would have cost." Tess smiled. She knew exactly how much a miracle costs—one dollar and eleven cents—plus the faith of a little child.

My friend, don't be afraid to ask your miracle-working God to work a miracle in your life. Don't allow stress to keep you from stepping out in faith. Remember that in God's economy, a miracle is not the suspension of natural law, but the operation of a higher law—grace.

A man in India was arraigned for stealing a lamb and was brought before the judge, as was another man who claimed to be the owner of the sheep. Both men had witnesses to prove their claim, making it difficult for the judge to decide which man was the lamb's true owner. Knowing, however, the custom of shepherds as well as the habits of the animal, the judge came up with a plan. He had the lamb brought into court, and sent one of the men into an adjoining room. He then instructed the remaining man to call the lamb. The poor animal, not knowing the voice of a stranger, wouldn't go to him. In the meantime, the other claimant, who was in an adjoining room, grew impatient. When he called the lamb, it immediately ran toward him. The judge immediately knew that he was the true owner of the lamb.

> When he brings all his sheep out, he goes ahead of them, and they follow him because they know his voice. But they will never follow a stranger. They will run away from him because they don't know his voice (John 10:4-5 NCV).

Grace filters every part of life through the love and faithfulness of God. When I graduated from college, I worked as a summer intern for a music and youth pastor in Dallas, Texas. That summer changed the direction of my life as I experienced, in a new way, the power of God working in and through me. One Sunday morning, the pastor called me into his office to let me know that the music and youth director with whom I worked was being fired immediately. I was devastated. Not only had this man and his family become precious friends, but his leaving meant that I was without a job and a church I had grown to love. In the shaky days ahead, I experienced the reality that God's grace really does cover everything. God eventually moved me to a church where I met an extraordinary young man named Dan Southerland. Not a day goes by that I don't thank God for the grace-filled trial that brought Dan and me together.

God's mercy provides a myriad of life experiences. Some we call good, some we call bad. But each one comes through a checkpoint of grace before it touches our lives. Paul was a man of grace.

> So that I would not become too proud of the wonderful things that were shown to me, a painful physical problem was given to me. This problem was a messenger from Satan, sent to beat me and keep me from being too proud. I begged the Lord three times to take this problem away from me. But he said to me, "My grace is enough for you. When you are weak, my power is made perfect in you." So I am very happy to brag about my weaknesses. Then Christ's power can live in me. For this reason, I am happy when I have weaknesses, insults, hard times, sufferings, and all kinds of troubles for Christ. Because when I am weak, then I am truly strong (2 Corinthians 12:7-10 NCV).

At some point in life we will find ourselves in a pit, desperately crying out for grace. We may have dug the pit with our own hands through wrong choices or it may be a pit hollowed out by the enemy. But a pit is a pit—dark, lonely, and filled with terror. The apostle Paul was certainly an illustration of God's life-changing grace, but he was also well acquainted with pits. In this passage, Paul reminds us that each pit is not only filled with the unknown but with the promises of God.

Promise One: There Is Purpose in the Pit

> So that I would not become too proud of the wonderful things that were shown to me, a painful physical problem was given to me. This problem was a messenger from Satan, sent to beat me and keep me from being too proud (2 Corinthians 12:7 NCV).

While every pit teems with stress, every pit also has a purpose, which means it comes to us for holy reasons.

Pits Come to Produce Balance

I have always thought of hurricanes as something mankind could do without, but I have recently learned that they are necessary to maintain a balance in nature. We know the devastation these storms can bring, yet scientists tell us they are tremendously valuable because they break up a large percentage of the oppressive heat which builds up at the equator and are indirectly responsible for much of the rainfall in North and South America. Consequently, meteorologists no longer resort to cloud-seeding techniques to prevent hurricanes from being formed. In fact, they are convinced that hurricanes actually do more good than harm.

Imbalance always produces stress, but God is always at work in our lives as the source of balance. If we had only blessings with which to contend, we would become fat, lazy, arrogant Christians. The principles of a balanced life are often forged through the fires of pain. The balance is found in the pit. The first four verses of 2 Corinthians 12 describe the incredible experience Paul had when he went to heaven. Now, I can't even begin to imagine what happened to Paul, and I don't want to get caught up in trying to figure out all of the details of his experience. Paul is simply telling us that he had an experience so awesome that it brought him nearer to God than he had ever been. It was the highest spiritual moment he had ever experienced, a moment when God honored Paul. Wow! This is big stuff—God honoring Paul. How could he possibly stay humble after having such an experience? Ah, yes. A pit. A pit is the perfect tool of balance between sorrow and joy, between darkness and light, between doubt and faith, between weakness and strength, between pride and humility. Proverbs 11:2 tells us "Pride leads only to shame; it is wise to be humble" (NCV). Life is like a prescription in that the individual ingredients may seem hurtful, but when correctly blended and balanced, will generate health.

Pits Come to Alter Perspective

An old legend says that at Creation, the birds felt cheated and hurt because they received wings. Wings appeared to be burdens that none of the other animals were asked to carry. Their perspective changed when they learned that wings weren't burdens at all, but blessings that allowed them to fly. Because they were given wings, they could rise above the earth to see sights that no other animal could see. What once seemed like burdens were really blessings.

Have you ever received a gift that you wanted to return but couldn't? I'm sure that Paul's first reaction was to take this so-called gift to the nearest Pit Store for a full refund. However, as he prayed about his problem, God showed him that it was actually a gift from God and had come to his life for good, for a higher purpose.

> The Lord says, "My thoughts are not like your thoughts. Your ways are not like my ways. Just as the heavens are higher than the earth, so are my ways higher than your ways and my thoughts higher than your thoughts" (Isaiah 55:8-9 NCV).

Pits change our perspective as they make us stop, reexamine priorities, and come face-to-face with our own insufficiency. Pits make us search for power beyond our own, and in doing so discover the all-sufficient power of God. Pits are good!

Pits Come to Strengthen Us

> For this reason I am happy when I have weaknesses, insults, hard times, sufferings, and all kinds of troubles for Christ. Because when I am weak, then I am truly strong (2 Corinthians 12:10 NCV).

The pits of life come to strengthen us. A beekeeper once explained how young bees are nurtured to ensure their healthy development. The queen lays each egg in a six-sided cell that is filled with enough pollen and honey to nourish the egg until it reaches a certain stage of maturity. The top is then sealed with a capsule of wax. When the food is gone, it's time for the tiny creature to be released! The wax is so hard to penetrate that the bee can make only a very narrow opening. It's so narrow that in the agony of exit, the bee rubs off the membrane encasing its wings. When the bee finally does emerge, it is able to fly! Occasionally, a moth will invade the hive to devour the wax capsules. As a result, the young bees crawl out with very little effort...but they cannot fly.

It is through the struggle of the trial and the climbing out of the pit that we become strong. Satan was allowed to attack Paul. The words "beat me" mean "to strike with the fist." The tense of the verb indicates that this pain was constant or recurring and was severe enough to affect Paul's ministry. "Thorn" means "a sharp stake used for torturing or impaling someone." Paul pleaded with God three times to remove the "thorn" from his life, but it remained. Paul tells us why. "When I am weak, then I am truly strong" (2 Corinthians 12:10 NCV). I love the words "truly strong" because they remind us that true strength truly comes from God. There is great purpose in every pit of life.

Promise Two: We Can Make a Choice About the Pit

When God allows suffering to touch our lives, we always have a choice to make. We can turn our anger toward Him and blame Him for the pain. We can choose to give up and wallow in the pit. We can don a religious smile, grit our spiritual teeth, and deny that the pit exists, or we can accept the pit. The choice to accept and even embrace the pain of the pits in life requires us to trust God, rest in Him, and walk in obedience.

Paul was not sinning when he asked God to remove his affliction. God tells us to do exactly what Paul did—bring our burdens to Him. "Give all your worries and cares to God, for he cares about what happens to you" (1 Peter 5:7 NLT). I admit that, given the stellar track record of Paul as a follower of Christ, I would have yanked that thorn right out of him as a reward for his faithfulness. But God said no. The fact that Paul asked three times makes me think he didn't fully understand God's refusal. Yet he made the choice to accept the pit as good. Paul may not have understood God's process, but he certainly trusted God's heart. And that was enough.

Promise Three: There Is Power in the Pit

> But he said to me, "My grace is enough for you. When you are weak, my power is made perfect in you." So I am very happy to brag about my weaknesses. Then Christ's power can live in me (2 Corinthians 12:9 NCV).

God sent a very important message to Paul and to us, a message of hope, power, and grace. The tense of the verb in this verse is very important. "But he said to me" can be translated, "He (God) has once-for-all said to me" and indicates a lifetime promise, an eternal promise that is wrapped around grace. God's grace is complete, sufficient, and never in short supply. God's grace always has our eternal good in mind.

The story is told of a businessman who was selling some warehouse property. The building had been empty for months and needed extensive repairs. Vandals had damaged the doors, smashed the windows, and thrown trash all over the floor. As he showed a prospective buyer the property, the businessman was careful to say that he would replace the broken windows, make any needed repairs, and clean up the place. The buyer stopped him and said, "Forget about the repairs. I'm going to build something completely different. I don't want the building; I just want the site." And that, my friend, is God's message of grace to us. When we come to God, the old life is over because He makes all things new. All the Father wants is the site and the permission to build.

> If anyone belongs to Christ; there is a new creation; the old is gone, the new has come! (2 Corinthians 5:17).

Grace transforms whatever it touches. Stress fades in the light of grace. People without Christ can marshal enough human courage and muster enough human strength to get through a trial. But God doesn't want us just to endure the hard times; He wants us to rise above them. Paul used his pain and made his trial work for him. As a result, God's power and peace were unleashed in Paul's life. The pit is both a burial place for stress and the birthplace for God's peace.

Promise Four: There Is Joy in the Pit

> I am very happy to brag about my weaknesses. Then Christ's power can live in me. For this reason I am happy when I have weaknesses, insults, hard times, sufferings, and all kinds of troubles for Christ (2 Corinthians 12: 9-10 NCV).

I truly believe God entrusts the greatest trials to those who will respond to them in the right way. The most joyful people I know are usually the ones who have suffered most because they have learned to count on God's promises instead of man's explanations. People who have learned to choose joy are walking trophies of grace. We cannot always find happiness in the pits of life, but we can always find joy.

Joy is not an earthly treasure but a heavenly gift from a loving Father who is committed to and loves His children. I love the story of the little girl who misquoted her favorite Bible verse: "For God so loved the world that He gave His only begotten Son so that whosoever believeth in Him should not perish, but have ever-laughing life!" Joy is why Jesus came; not just to give us life but to give us a life of joy—pits and all. Remember two important truths about joy:

- Joy is the deeply-rooted confidence that God is in control.
- Your inward attitudes do not have to reflect your outer circumstances.

Dr. Viktor Frankl, author of the book *Man's Search for Meaning* was imprisoned by the Nazis in World War II because he was a Jew. His wife, children, and parents were all killed in the Holocaust. The Gestapo made him strip and stand totally naked before them. As they cut away his wedding band, Viktor said to himself, "You can take away my wife and my children and strip away my clothes. You can destroy everything that I possess, but there is one thing that no person can ever take away from me. You can never take my freedom to choose how I will react to what happens to me."

You may find yourself in a frightening place. The stress of the day may be closing in on you. Your greatest dream may have become your worst nightmare. Your bewildered heart may be wondering if God even knows or cares where you are or what you need. Let me assure you my friend—He does. Don't think for a minute that just because you can't see the hand of God or sense His presence that it means He is not working. Nothing could be further from the truth. The grace of God is *always* at work in our lives. You can count on it.

Stress-Busters

From Ellen and Sally

Forgive yourself, begin each day anew, and work toward making better decisions today than yesterday. Here are some guidelines that will help you make better food choices:

- 5 days on, 2 days off—Eat well Sunday afternoon to Friday afternoon. Enjoy some treats on the weekend.

- Shoot for a pattern of eating 60 to 70 percent God-made foods. You will be on the upside of a healthy diet.

- Enjoy at least three different God-made colored foods at each meal—and not just white, beige, and brown. The deeper darker the colors, the better. Blueberries are best!

○ ○ ○

- I work at keeping a clear purpose and a balanced schedule, finding support from Christian friends, and having times of self-examination. My favorite stress-busters are John 10:10 and Colossians 2:10.

- To relieve minor stresses, I listen to classical music because there are no words to focus on. Some music makes me want to sing while some music can actually be stressful!

- To relieve major stresses, I'm learning the simple art of saying no. Sometimes, it's a "No, thank you" or "I'm sorry, but no" or "No, not now." I try to wrap my "no" in an appropriate way, depending on what/who I'm saying no to, but at the center of it is a definite "no."

- Sit outside in the hot tub on a chilly night under the stars.

- Fly a kite or have a tea party with a child.

- Watch a funny movie.

- Go to the park and feed the ducks. While you are there, hit the swings.

- Journaling is good spiritual therapy. Write down all of your stress-filled thoughts and feelings. Then leave them all in God's hands…and close the book.

- Wear comfortable and loose clothing and take off your shoes when possible.

- Avoid holding in feelings day after day. Instead, find a safe place to feel, express, and embrace them.

- Do one thing at a time.

- Give up on perfection, a huge source of stress.

- Get to know yourself. Acknowledge your likes and dislikes, strengths and weaknesses. What are your values and ideals? How does your body tell you when you are stressed or tired? How do you behave when stressed?

9

Take the Long Look

I will dwell in the house of the LORD forever.
PSALM 23:6 NKJV

El Olam: *The Everlasting God*

~ The Shepherd and His Sheep ~

Shepherding is a lifetime commitment for both the shepherd and the sheep. Because the shepherd is committed to the complete care of his sheep, he is always focused on both seen and unseen dangers. Even the possibility of harm is taken into account by the shepherd who, before the danger comes, makes a way of escape. Since hyenas, jackals, wolves, and even bears are common and feed on sheep, the shepherds often have to do battle with these wild and dangerous beasts. A shepherd literally has to put his life on the line while defending his sheep. He is their only hope.

○ ○ ○

I love the story of a middle-aged man taking a Caribbean cruise.

On his first day out, he noticed an attractive woman about his own age who gave him a friendly smile as he passed her on the deck. Pleased, he managed to get seated at the same dinner table that night. As they talked, he commented that he had seen her on the deck that day and thought she had a beautiful smile. The woman responded, "Well, I must confess the reason I smiled. You see, when I saw you, I was immediately struck by your strong resemblance to my third husband." A bit surprised, the man replied, "Really! How many times have you been married?" With a shy smile, the woman softly said, "Twice." Now there is a woman who majored in hope, choosing to live each day in the light of every tomorrow and the possibilities the future might hold. To deal with stress, we must do the same.

We all have hopes and expectations that motivate us and, at times, keep us going. However, we tend to put our hope in things we can see and have confidence in things we can explain! The psalmist writes, "We wait in hope for the LORD; he is our help and our shield" (Psalm 33:20). Until the issue of eternity is settled, there can be no hope. A personal relationship with Jesus Christ fills every unknown with peace. Uncertainty and stress cannot stand up to the power of God. As James writes, if we know and follow God, we can face whatever tomorrow holds with peace and confidence.

> Come now, you who say, "Today or tomorrow we will go to such and such a town and spend a year there, buy and sell, and make a profit"; whereas you do not know what will happen tomorrow. For what is your life? It is even a vapor that appears for a little time and then vanishes away. Instead you ought to say, "If the Lord wills, we shall live and do this or that." But now you boast in your arrogance. All such boasting is evil. Therefore, to him who knows to do good and does not do it, to him it is sin (James 4:13-17 NKJV).

Most of us take the future for granted, assuming that the plans and routines of today will bring about the desired results and fervent hopes of tomorrow. As I mentioned earlier, Dan and I have been married and in ministry together for 30 years. From day one, life has been neither dull nor boring. In fact, there have been times when I silently longed for just one unexciting day, concluding that boredom is highly underrated. Looking back, the days were filled with the normal routines we call life...marriage, ministry, family, children, school, and work. At times we made plans, but honestly, we often took the future for granted.

My perspective of tomorrow was radically altered several years ago when I had to rush my husband to the hospital. Dan had not felt well for a couple of days, but we chalked it up to the stomach flu going around. After preaching four services, he came home, claimed the couch, confiscated the remote control, and announced that he would soon be well. Instead, his nausea graduated into excruciating pain. When I declared that we were going to the emergency room... and he agreed...I knew something was seriously wrong with my husband, who avoided hospitals and doctors whenever possible.

Now I must confess I have been known to drive fast from time to time. I prefer to describe my method of driving as "quick." However, as I drove Dan to the hospital, I added "flying" to my repertoire of driving techniques, a fact that was not overlooked by the policeman who attempted to wave me over for a landing after I ran a red light and pulled out in front of him. I actually did stop long enough to jump out of my car and yell, "I do *not* have time for this! I'm taking my husband to the hospital!" Satisfied that I had provided all the information the officer needed, I climbed back into the car and took off. A quick glance in the rearview mirror confirmed my assumption that the policeman understood the situation as his flailing arms motioned me onward and his shouts of encouragement filled the air. Sometimes, ignorance really is bliss.

Dan was immediately admitted to the hospital for tests that soon revealed a burst appendix instead of the heart attack I had feared due to his long history of high blood pressure. My relief was short-lived. Every operating room was full. My husband would have to wait. As Dan's temperature began to climb, his pain became unmanageable and so did I. Stepping into the hallway, I cried out to God. He heard. Minutes later, the surgeon walked in, took one look at Dan, and instructed the nurses to take him to surgery immediately! Go, God!

The waiting room filled with family and friends. Tears mixed with laughter and prayer as we encouraged one another and waited. After what seemed like an eternity, the surgeon stepped into the room and said, "Mary, the surgery went well, and I think Dan is going to be fine." It was the word "think" that bothered me, but he quickly went on to explain. "The appendix had evidently burst several hours before surgery because there was a great deal of infection that I did not anticipate. We have him on massive doses of antibiotics and will keep him in the hospital for a few days just in case." I am convinced there is a mandatory class in medical school that teaches doctors what to say and how to say it so that you are left dangling on the edge of terror. Dan was a very sick man for several days, but thankfully he made a full recovery. As I sat by his bed, the hours filled with haunting reflections of what-if. God reminded me that my hope must be placed in Him alone. Not my husband. Not doctors. Not my plans for the future. He led me to pinpoint some very important truths about how to face tomorrow with confidence and hope instead of doubt and fear.

Truth One: Recognize That Life Is Short

> What is your life? It is even a vapor that appears for a little time and then vanishes away (James 4:14 NKJV).

Life is as temporary as a fog that quickly and silently disappears. While on vacation in North Carolina, we soon learned to expect fog every morning...even in the summer. One chilly morning we set out to see the beautiful colonial home of Carl Sandburg on the Blue Ridge Parkway. The closer we got, the denser was the fog. When we arrived, the fog was so thick we could see very little. Disappointed, we asked the owner of the gift shop when would be a good time to come back. With a smile he said, "Just wait an hour and the fog will be gone." I looked outside at the thick haze and thought, "There is no way. That fog is going to last all day." Nevertheless, we shopped for an hour and when we walked out of the gift shop, the fog was beginning to lift. Soon the skies were crystal clear and the sun was shining as if the haze had never existed.

Life is much the same—temporary and fleeting. Stress comes when we refuse to accept the fact that life is indeed short. Most of us live as if tomorrow will never come, putting off dreams and postponing goals. We race headlong through each day because, after all, there *is* always tomorrow. Our intentions are good. We have simply forgotten that life is short.

> So we do not look at what we can see right now, the troubles all around us, but we look forward to the joys in heaven which we have not yet seen. The troubles will soon be over, but the joys to come will last forever (2 Corinthians 4:18 TLB).

It's so easy to get caught up in putting out insignificant fires, handling the ordinary moments and situations until we look up one day and this life is over. Live each day as if it were your last. Make every moment count. Keep a "forever" perspective because life really is short.

Truth Two: Admit We Are Blind

> Why, you do not even know what will happen tomorrow (James 4:14).

We are all blind about tomorrow, a limitation that is both universal and unquestionable. The only thing we do know about tomorrow is that it will be different from today. Not necessarily better or worse, but definitely different. As a result, I believe our biggest problem with tomorrow is a control issue. Let's face it. We are control freaks. Because we desperately want to call all of the shots, we spend today trying somehow to control tomorrow. When we feel that control slipping through our hands, we stress out.

A weary Christian lay awake, trying to hold the world together by his incessant worrying. After pouring out all of his fear and anxiety to God in prayer, he heard the Father gently say, "Now you go to sleep, Jim. I'll sit up."

When it comes to tomorrow, we are blind. That reality will not change this side of heaven. But neither will the truth that God holds every tomorrow in the palm of His hand.

> My frame was not hidden from you when I was made in the secret place. When I was woven together in the depths of the earth, your eyes saw my unformed body. All the days ordained for me were written in your book before one of them came to be (Psalm 139:15-16).

Truth Three: Avoid Presumption About Tomorrow

> Come now, you who say, "Today or tomorrow we will go to such and such a city and spend a year there and engage in business and make a profit" (James 4:13 NASB).

> As it is, you boast in your arrogance; all such boasting is evil (James 4:16 NASB).

James paints a scenario here that I believe you and I will find very familiar. It's the picture of the typical, goal-oriented businessman, living by the book, his daily planner. Stress is written across every page. He appears to be an extremely organized and motivated salesman with very specific plans.

- He was self-assertive in his travel plans ("we will go to this or that city").
- He was self-confident in his time schedule ("spend a year there").
- He was self-centered in his goals ("carry on business and make money").

Arrogance is at the heart of this man and too often fills our hearts as well. We order our days, make our schedules, and then, as an afterthought, ask the Father to join us in our wonderful plan when what we really need to do is seek Him and join Him in His plan. A right attitude toward God requires total abandonment to God.

> Don't brag about what will happen tomorrow
> (Proverbs 27:1 ICB).

> We can make our plans, but the LORD determines our steps
> (Proverbs 16:9 NLT).

James is not saying that it's wrong to plan and organize or unspiritual to set goals and go after them. He is, however, shining a ruthless light on the heart attitude behind those goals, reminding us that our tomorrows belong to the One who holds them.

Truth Four: Do What You Know to Do Today

> To one who knows the right thing to do, and does not do it,
> to him it is sin (James 4:17 NASB).

Knowledge equals responsibility. Procrastination is sin and one of the greatest sources of stress in life. I once heard a preacher tell the old story of three demons who were arguing over the best way to destroy the Christian movement. The first demon had it all figured out. "Let's tell all the Christians there is no heaven. If we take away the reward incentive, their movement will collapse." The second demon responded with, "No, I have a better idea. Let's tell all of the Christians that there really is no hell. If we take away their fear of punishment, their movement will collapse." The third demon offered, "Both of those are great ideas, but there is a better way. Let's tell all the Christians that there is no hurry!" The other demons applauded in delight! "That's it!" they said. "Our best weapon of all is procrastination."

Truth is for now. God is not impressed with good intentions.

Obedience today is the greatest preparation for tomorrow's trials. What I am capable of tomorrow is contained in who I am and what I do today.

> The thing you should want most is God's kingdom and doing what God wants. Then all these other things you need will be given to you. So don't worry about tomorrow, because tomorrow will have its own worries. Each day has enough trouble of its own (Matthew 6:33-34 NCV).

Hope is always found in obedience to God. Consequently, sin erodes hope and produces a stress that can only be dealt with through repentance followed by obedience. When we confess sin, God not only forgives that sin but removes the stain it leaves behind. The stain of sin is one of Satan's favorite weapons in the war with stress. With it, he births guilt and shame, crippling us spiritually. Obedience empowers us to live in peace, with stress under His control.

Do what you know to do today. The Proverbs 31 woman did. In fact, Scripture tells us she could "laugh at the days to come" (Proverbs 31:25). In other words, this woman fully lived in the present but carefully planned and prepared for the future. Proverbs 31:19 indicates that she made thread with her hands and weaved her own cloth: "In her hand she holds the distaff and grasps the spindle with her fingers." Notice she only made thread and cloth—not the finished product of clothes. That was a task for the future. She was simply getting ready today to meet the needs of tomorrow. The result was a life filled with hope and lived out in purpose.

She Saved

With money she earned (Proverbs 31:16 NCV).

The Proverbs 31 woman worked hard, saved her earnings, and then invested her financial gain wisely. Money is a powerful resource but also one of life's greatest stress producers.

Jesus talked a lot about money. Of the 38 parables Jesus told, 16 of them teach how to handle money and possessions. The Bible has 500 verses on prayer, less than 500 verses on faith, and more than 2000 verses on money. How we handle our financial resources is a part of spiritual discipline and an essential determining factor in our stress level.

A budget is a spiritual document that illustrates whom or what we worship. The Proverbs 31 woman worked to meet her immediate financial needs. She was not only a successful businesswoman but also a successful wife and mother who provided well for her family.

The Proverbs 31 woman dressed well and seemed to enjoy the finer things of life. There is nothing wrong with living comfortably, dressing well, or driving a nice car—unless the price is too high. If financial accomplishments come at the cost of too much debt, if it comes out of a spirit of discontent and keeps us from giving, if it interferes with family priorities, then living well becomes very wrong. Hebrews 13:5 warns, "Keep your lives free from the love of money and be satisfied with what you have. God has said, "I will never leave you; I will never forget you" (NCV). We often read the first part of that verse and never get to the heart of its truth. Contentment is not the result of having what we want. Contentment is the result of wanting what we have.

She Planted

> She plants a vineyard (Proverbs 31:16 NCV).

It takes years for a vineyard to yield a crop. By planting a vineyard, the Proverbs 31 woman was preparing for and making an investment in the future. The message here is that in every area of life, we need to plant the right seeds today in order to produce the right crop tomorrow.

Vineyards take constant care, diligent attention, and careful planning. Our lives are filled with many types of vineyards. Our spiritual vineyard requires daily nourishment found through time spent in the Word of God and at the feet of Jesus in prayer. The vineyard of family requires faithful love, chosen forgiveness, supernatural patience, and a commitment to see the "crop" through to the harvest. We tend to neglect the physical, emotional, and mental vineyards of life in order to concentrate on those fields we deem more important, a choice that always results in more stress. The apostle Paul states that "people harvest only what they plant" (Galatians 6:7 NCV) and that "the person who plants a little will have a small harvest, but the person who plants a lot will have a big harvest" (2 Corinthians 9:6 NCV). The sobering reality is that our vineyards will produce whatever we plant in them.

Years ago, a young black child was growing up in Cleveland where his home was materially poor but spiritually rich. One day, a famous athlete named Charlie Paddock came to his school to speak to the students. At that time, Paddock was considered "the fastest human being alive." He asked the students, "What do you want to be? You name it; then believe that God will help you be it!" The little boy decided he wanted to be the fastest man alive. He went to his track coach and announced his new dream. His coach told him, "It's great to have a dream, but to attain that dream you have to build a ladder to it. Here is the ladder to your dream. The first rung is determination. The second rung is commitment. The third rung is discipline, and the fourth rung is attitude." That young boy went on to win four gold medals in the 1936 Berlin Olympics. He won the 100-meter dash and broke the Olympic and world records for the 200 meter. His name was Jesse Owens, and his life was the fruit of some well-planted and well-nourished seeds.

The psalmist writes that we were created for eternity. "I will dwell in the house of the LORD forever" (Psalm 23:6). Instead of focusing on "forever" things, we waste precious emotional energy and priceless spiritual power by fixing our gaze on the here and now. I'm not saying we need to ignore what God gives us to do today, because the truth is that each step on each day's path is filled with God-ordained opportunities. What I *am* saying is that much of our stress comes when we measure life against the wrong backdrop.

We must be very careful to choose the right backdrop against which we live and love and serve. Our backdrop is eternity, not the tyranny of urgent demands made by a relentless world. Our backdrop is an old rugged cross, not the condemnation of our own hearts and the hearts of others. Our backdrop is an empty tomb, not the stress-filled prison of hopelessness. My favorite words in the Bible are "But God..." Those two words create an eternal backdrop that changes everything. Everything looks different when He comes. Everything is made different by God's presence. When we stop and take a long look, life will be the abundant existence God meant it to be and stress will give way to peace. Does that mean we will float through each day without facing trials, defeats, enemies, or impossibilities? No. It simply means that the backdrop against which we view those dark moments will be replaced with the truth that God is enough.

When stress threatens and it seems as though you can't go on, rest in God's truth and take the long look at life, knowing that He will provide your every need and fill your heart with peace.

Stress-Busters

From Ellen and Sally

Take the long look. God created your amazing physical machine for a purpose. It is so complex that not even ten percent of your brain is used. Your potential is staggering. You must keep your body working efficiently for optimal performance. To do less is irresponsible. To do less is to dishonor God's work.

Because we are not perfect, God has invented physiological backups to thwart a reasonable amount of behavioral and physical abuse. Your immune and endocrine systems protect and repair your organs. White blood cells fight the bad cells. Your brain is wired with alarm systems such as fevers to warn you to take healing action. Your heart speeds up when under stress to deliver needed nutrients. Your liver takes care of toxins. There are many ways your body eliminates body pollutants. However, there is a point when your body says, "Enough! I can't handle this overload any more." Then something breaks down, causing you to take an unplanned hiatus. Illness, especially serious illness, is debilitating. You may grow more spiritually during this time, but why go there if you can prevent it by fueling your temple with God-made foods? It's simple—eat God-made foods for your God-made body!

○ ○ ○

- Ask yourself: Tomorrow, will this really matter? In a month, will this really matter? If the answer is yes, take appropriate action. If the answer is no, why are you worrying and getting stressed about it? Let it go.

- Don't rely on your memory. Write down appointments and make a list of tasks that must be completed during the week. Then divide the list, assigning certain tasks to certain days.

- Keep a duplicate car and house key in your wallet and give a copy to your neighbor.

- An instant cure for most stress: thirty minutes of brisk walking or any other aerobic exercise.

- Set up contingency plans—just in case. "If we get separated in the mall, here's what we'll do…"

- For every one thing that goes wrong, there are 50 to 100 blessings. Count them and focus on them.

- Learn to live one day at a time.

- Every day, do at least one thing you really enjoy.

- Don't sweat the small stuff.

- Remember that the best things in life aren't things.

- Change is stressful. Whenever there's a major change in your life, look for any opportunities the new situation offers.

- It really does help to talk to someone. Build a network of supportive family and friends. If you don't feel comfortable talking to anyone close to you, talk to a counselor.

- Being a good listener is one of life's important skills; listening helps prevent misunderstanding and helps build friendships. Poor communication is a major cause of stress, so learn how to talk, write, and listen effectively.

- Pay attention to the health of your relationships. Make good connections with family and friends. Be willing to accept and give help. A strong support group is essential to stress management.

A Few Final Thoughts

Stress has been tenacious in its quest to derail and damage my life, trapping me in its vicious cycle of devastation and waste. If I'm not careful, it will make me stumble and fall right back into the pit of clinical depression. I have already been there, done that, and have no desire to go back. Many marriages, homes, and lives are teetering on the brink of disaster because we are too busy. Personal and family needs are consigned to the bottom of our priority list—and the enemy stands in the shadows, laughing and applauding our foolishness. Distractions are rampant because our lives are not focused. Stop. Get off of the merry-go-round. Come into God's presence and rest there until stress has gone and peace has come.

A lecturer, when explaining stress management to an audience, raised a glass of water and asked, "How heavy is this glass of water?" Answers ranged from five ounces to twenty ounces. The lecturer went on, "The absolute weight doesn't matter. It depends on how long you try to hold it. I can hold the glass for one minute with no problem. If I hold it for an hour, my right arm will ache. However, if I hold the glass of water for an entire day, you will have to call an ambulance. In each case, it is the same weight, but the longer I hold it, the heavier it becomes."

The same is true of stress. The longer we hold onto stress, the heavier it becomes. Stress that is dealt with incorrectly can lead to physical illness, emotional bankruptcy, and a hay-and-stubble existence void of power and strength.

Let me challenge you to read Psalm 23 every day for a month and then check your stress level. Don't be afraid to cry out for help. Take time to evaluate and realign your priorities. Don't allow yourself to become wrapped up in anything or anyone but God. And may His peace follow you all the days of your life! Amen.

Bible Study Guide

Chapter One: Know Whose You Are

Key verses:

> All Scripture is inspired by God and is useful to teach us what is true and to make us realize what is wrong in our lives. It straightens us out and teaches us to do what is right. It is God's way of preparing us in every way, fully equipped for every good thing God wants us to do (2 Timothy 3:16-17 NLT).

Key truths:

If we really want to know God, and whose we are, the Bible must have the highest place of authority in our lives. We don't have to be Bible scholars or have a firm grip on the Hebrew and Greek languages to know and apply God's promises. As you read the Bible, the Holy Spirit will give you new understanding and teach you spiritual truth. He will then give you the power you need to follow those teachings and apply their truths.

A disciple of God is a learner and a student of the ways of God. We must understand the importance of the Bible, love it, and spend time in it. I thought I was doing a fair job of plugging the truth of God's Word into my life until I began to gather Scripture for this chapter and rammed right into Psalm 119. Within this passage, I discovered a test for us as believers that will help determine the importance we really place on God's Word. Take this test with me to see if God's Word has the place in your life it should have.

1. Is God's Word more important than food?

> Your promises are sweet to me, sweeter than honey in my mouth (Psalm 119:103 NCV).

In this verse the Bible is described as honey and in other passages of Scripture as milk or bread. Simply put, the Bible is our spiritual food. God's Word sustains and strengthens us in the same way that food sustains and strengthens our physical body. Just as malnutrition affects our physical growth, spiritual malnutrition affects our spiritual growth. Oh, we rarely miss a meal. We always find a way to eat. Do we have the same depth of commitment to our spiritual growth and health as we do to satisfying the hunger pains of our human body?

2. Is God's Word more important than money?

> Your teachings are worth more to me than thousands of pieces of gold and silver (Psalm 119:72 NCV).

The psalmist is saying that spiritual wealth is more important than human wealth. Do we really live as if that statement were true? I have a friend who is totally committed to God and to serving Him wholeheartedly. My friend is a garbage collector—a happy garbage collector. I once asked him why he was so content in his work. "Mary, I collect garbage to pay the bills but my *real* passion in life is to share Jesus Christ and to serve Him with joy." I recently spoke at a church that is almost totally staffed by volunteers. One couple in particular felt led to serve the church but knew that the church budget could not handle another salary. What did they do? They moved into a tiny, one-bedroom apartment and sold their car to buy a smaller, more economical vehicle. The husband quit his job to work as a full-time volunteer at the church and his wife took a church staff position paying a minimal salary that they both live on. I have never met two happier or less-stressed people. They have the right backdrop for life, and it is neither wealth nor money.

3. Is God's Word more important to you than sleep?

> I wake up early in the morning and cry out. I hope in your word. I stay awake all night so I can think about your promises (Psalm 119:147-148 NCV).

Now God is getting personal. When we start talking about giving up sleep to read and study the Word of God, we are talking radical obedience. Exactly. If we want to experience God's power in our lives, we have to saturate our lives with His Word.

How did you do? I will tell you honestly that I failed this test. I've walked with God for more than 40 years, and I *still* don't have the hunger and thirst for God's Word that I should have. If we listen carefully, I believe we could hear God say, "If you want to get to know Me—really know Me—if you want to be intimate with Me, then you have to know My Book." The level of stress in my life is directly correlated to the amount of time I spend or don't spend reading and applying the Word of God.

We find a way to do the things in life that are important to us. We are driven to work in order to live the good life, but we neglect the most important—the only eternal part of our being—our soul. Our soul can only be nourished and fed by the Word of the Living God. How important is God's Word in your life?

> Does a maiden forget her jewelry, a bride her wedding ornaments? Yet my people have forgotten me, days without number (Jeremiah 2:32).

I can hear the sorrow in God's words, can't you? They vividly portray the broken heart of a Father whose children have ignored Him and abandoned His ways. I know what it does to me as a parent when my children don't listen to me or when they choose a path that is in direct opposition to one that I would have chosen for them. I can only imagine what it does to the heart of God when we go for days and even weeks or months without even picking up the Bible except as an accessory for others to see when attending church.

We live in Charlotte, North Carolina, where Union Power Company makes a tremendous amount of electricity available to us. With that power we can light our homes and stay warm in the winter and cool in the summer. We can enjoy electrically powered appliances that turn, spin, wash, dry, and clean. Electricity makes a huge difference in our lives…when we flip the switch. But unless we use and appropriate the power of available electricity, it is worthless to us. The same is true of the Bible.

Application steps:

Set aside one hour this week to reevaluate your plan for reading and studying God's Word. Set new goals for daily Bible study. Make the goals realistic for your current lifestyle. Next week, add 15 minutes to your daily study time. Ask the Father to empower this new commitment. Set a specific time and place for your Bible study. Remember to record new truths and insights in a journal and at the end of the week, go back over your entries to see what changes God has made in your life. Praise Him for the power of His Word. When you fail, do not allow the enemy to discourage you or persuade you to give up. Simply begin again.

Memory verse:

All scripture is God-breathed and is useful for teaching, rebuking, correcting and training in righteousness, so that the man of God may be thoroughly equipped for every good work (2 Timothy 3:16).

Reflection point:

"The level of stress in my life is directly correlated to the amount of time I spend or don't spend reading and applying the Word of God." In your journal, record any thoughts, ideas, or new perspectives you have in response to this statement.

Power verses:

My sheep hear My voice, and I know them, and they follow Me; and I give eternal life to them, and they will never perish; and no one shall snatch them out of my Hand (John 10:27-28).

He takes care of his people like a shepherd. He gathers them like lambs in his arms and carries them close to him. He gently leads the mothers of the lambs (Isaiah 40:11 NCV).

Hear the word of the LORD, O nations; proclaim it in distant coastlands: "He who scattered Israel will gather them and will watch over his flock like a shepherd" (Jeremiah 31:10).

One new truth: _____

_____

_____

My prayer for today:

Father, I pray You would give me a hunger and thirst for Your Word. I want to please You with my life through my obedience to Your truths. I choose to spend time with You each day this week, reading and studying the Bible. Would You please honor my commitment and empower me to keep it? When I fail, Lord, I choose now to forgive myself as You forgive me—and begin again. Thank You for the Bible and the power it holds. May that power be seen in me for Your glory. Amen.

Chapter Two: Recognize Your Source

Key verse:

> Tell those who are rich in this world not to be proud and not
> to trust in their money, which will soon be gone. But their
> trust should be in the living God, who richly gives us all we
> need for our enjoyment (1 Timothy 6:17).

Key truths:

Through the years, the mountains of North Carolina have always been a favorite vacation spot for our family. I recall one summer in particular when Jered was nine and Danna was six years old. We had heard so much about Grandfather Mountain and decided that the kids were finally old enough to handle the physical demands of such an adventurous climb. A stop at the local mall was in order since both kids needed new shoes. Danna chose a pair of pink slip-on canvas sneakers while Jered opted for traditional sports shoes. We were ready to go. The level of excitement grew as our faithful old van wound its way up the mountain to the visitors center. The kids jumped out, yelling for us to hurry, ready for the quest to begin!

The first leg of the expedition required us to cross a high, swinging bridge in order to enjoy the most spectacular view offered by Grandfather Mountain. With the confidence of veteran climbers, we traipsed across the bridge with ease and in absolute awe of the mountainous beauty. We sat gazing at the stunning display of God's handiwork and the splendor of His creation strewn before us. None of us really wanted to move from our scenic overlook, but the crowd grew larger by the moment and a cold wind started picking up, so we decided it was time to go. Reluctantly, we began walking back to the van. It was then that we spotted the sign. Hiking trails were just ahead. And we love to hike.

Just before the starting point of the climb, we passed a large wooden billboard warning all hikers to make sure they were fully equipped for the trails ahead, listing necessities like water, food, hiking gear, and first aid kits. When I pointed out the sign to my husband, he said, "Honey, that sign is *not* for Southerlands!" Of course. What was I thinking?

Sauntering right past the billboard's caution and all sanity, we embarked on what seemed to be a very nice and easy climb—until we came to an ambiguous fork in the path. There were no maps or signs and not a single person to guide us. We were contemplating which path to take when a group of college students came rambling down one of the mountain paths, talking, laughing, and obviously having a great time. They were clearly excited about the climb they had just made and seemed almost refreshed, without so much as a drop of perspiration between them. We asked if the trail they had just taken would be easy enough for the kids. Taking a scrutinizing look at our young, canvas-shod children accompanied by their two ill-equipped parents, these students assured us that we could handle the hike with no problems at all. Off we went.

It wasn't long before we realized that we were in serious trouble. The path grew harder and steeper. We met fewer and fewer climbers until it seemed as if we were the only ones left on the mountain. I remember thinking, "Tell me again, Lord, why I married this man?" On we climbed—scaling huge boulders and finding ourselves on an extremely narrow path that skirted a deadly drop of several hundred feet. At one point, Dan and I were literally planting each child's foot in a safe place, holding them steady in order to prevent a fall off of the mountain. With every step, my panic grew until we rounded the mountaintop and the last boulder loomed in front of us. It was enormous, but, oh, it was a thing of beauty! You see, someone had been there before us and bolted metal stakes into the side of the boulder, forming a ladder we could use to scale the massive rock, reach the other side, and find the path down the mountain. We finished the climb, realizing that God does indeed take care of the faithful and the foolish, as well as those of us who vacillate in between.

Driving home, the perfect provision of God's plan for the day and for my life swept over me in sweet relief. Just as surely as God took care of us on that mountain, He takes care of us every minute of every day. The victories of yesterday are spiritual markers for the journey today. God is faithful, and He repeatedly proves that promise to us. "He is good and His mercy endures forever" the psalmist proclaims (Psalm 106:1). If God came through yesterday, He will come through today. If God was faithful yesterday, He will be faithful today. His love never changes, He holds each tomorrow in the palm of His hand, and He has gone before us, through the darkness of every trial and over each mountain erected by the circumstances of life, making a way. He is the Way-Maker where there is no way. Rejoice, my friend. Refuse stress and choose to rest in the truth that God is your source and that He is enough!

Application steps:

- Give something in secret this week, expecting nothing in return.
- Take inventory of your stuff, making a tangible list.
- Set aside time this week to give each item on that list to God.
- Praise God for His abundance in your life.

Memory verse:

> A greedy person causes trouble, but the one who trusts the LORD will succeed (Proverbs 28:25 NCV).

Reflection points:

I need to understand that greed will destroy my peace and contentment. As I examine my life, I ask the Holy Spirit to reveal every area of greed to me. I confess my greed as sin and choose against it. I choose to look for ways to practice kingdom giving.

Power verses:

> Tell them to use their money to do good. They should be rich in good works and should give generously to those in need, always being ready to share with others whatever God has given them (1 Timothy 6:18 NLT).

> Among you there must not be even a hint of sexual immorality, or of any kind of impurity, or of greed, because these are improper for God's holy people (Ephesians 5:3).

> You are my refuge and my shield; your word is my only source of hope (Psalm 119:114 NLT).

One new truth: _____

_____

_____

My prayer for today:

Father, I confess to You that my heart is often filled with greed. Forgive me for assigning such importance to material things. Right now I surrender every possession to You and choose against envy and the lust for material things. Today I choose to focus on what I have instead of what I want. Please fill my heart with Your motives and Your giving spirit. Amen.

Chapter Three: Know When to Rest

Key verse:

> Teach us to make the most of our time, so that we may grow in wisdom (Psalm 90:12 NLT).

Key truths:

Every minute of every day is either wasted or invested. Since the Bible contains more than 400 verses about time, we can safely assume that time management is important to God and is, in fact, a spiritual discipline. We not only need to view time as an eternal investment, but as an immediate one as well. One of the most valuable investments we can make is to spend time in solitude.

I once read an African proverb and prayer, "Lord Jesus, make my heart sit down." Solitude is deliberately and diligently setting aside time to "sit down" at the feet of Jesus. It's in those still, quiet moments at His feet that we hear God's voice and gain strength and wisdom for the journey ahead. In order to practice solitude, we must learn how to budget time.

It's been said that women must balance their time more carefully than men because women don't have wives. The fact is we're all responsible for how we spend the time God has given us. Time is a precious gift! Every morning we are credited with 86,400 seconds. No balance is carried into the next day and every night erases what we fail to use. If we use it in the wrong way, that time is lost forever and cannot be reclaimed. Unbudgeted time gravitates to our weaknesses, is stolen by others, or wasted on the unimportant. We must budget time, just as Jesus did.

At the age of 12, Jesus traveled to Jerusalem with His parents for the annual Passover Celebration. When His parents began the long trip home, they didn't miss Him at first, and when they did, they assumed He was traveling with friends.

Jesus was found in the temple, teaching. My first reaction would probably have been pride in the fact that religious scholars and veteran teachers were actually listening to my young son. I would most likely have encouraged Jesus to continue, basking in the looming recognition and acclaim. Instead, Jesus returned home where, for 18 to 20 years, He simply grew. Luke 2:52 tells us Jesus grew mentally, physically, spiritually, and socially. In Luke 3, Jesus begins His ministry, the most powerful ministry ever known. In other words, Jesus Christ budgeted His time wisely, resulting in a balanced life of fulfilled purpose. We can live the same kind of life—if our priorities are right.

Set priorities:

Ecclesiastes 3:1 tells us "there is a time for everything, and a season for every activity under heaven" (NLT). We either set our life priorities or allow circumstances and other people to set them.

Schedule priorities:

There is a right time and a right way to carry out right priorities. Ecclesiastes 8:5-6 warns, "A wise heart knows the proper time and procedure. For there is a proper time and procedure for every delight" (NASB). We must schedule time for solitude. We must set aside portions of each day to spend with God.

Stick to priorities:

The apostle Paul teaches us to make "the most of every opportunity" (Ephesians 5:16). Every challenge will either wreck our priorities or affirm them. Right priorities stand firm in the face of change.

One day, we will all stand before the Father and give an account of how we invested our time. Today, examine your time management habits in light of eternity. Initiate schedule changes that honor God. Make a new commitment to invest your time wisely.

Application steps:

- Choose to practice solitude—today.

- Select a place to spend time in solitude—today.
- Lay down your agenda.
- Focus on God and listen for His voice.

Memory verse:

> Be still before the LORD and wait patiently for him
> (Psalm 37:7).

Reflection points:

Ask yourself these questions and use the answers to shape a plan for regular solitude:

- Why am I afraid of silence?
- What is the greatest obstacle to solitude in my life?
- What steps do I have to take in order to remove those obstacles?
- What do I hope to gain from time spent in solitude?

Power verses:

> Come to me, all you who are weary and burdened, and I will give you rest (Matthew 11:28).

> On the seventh day God rested from all his work (Hebrews 4:4).

One new truth: _____

_____

_____

My prayer for today:

Father, I recognize my need for time alone with You. I lay down my schedule, my agenda, and anything else in my life that would keep me from that time. Please forgive me for the way I often squander away the minutes, hours, and days of my life. Give me the power to invest time wisely and the wisdom to live a balanced life. Amen.

Chapter Four: Do What God Gives You to Do

Key verse:

> Never be lazy in your work, but serve the Lord enthusiastically (Romans 12:11 NLT).

Key truths:

God uses our work to mold us into who He wants us to be. Stress comes when we view our job as our main life mission when, in reality, work provides the tools we need to accomplish our life mission. Paul writes, "Life is worth nothing unless I use it for doing the work assigned me by the Lord Jesus—the work of telling others the Good News about God's mighty kindness and love" (Acts 20:24 TLB). Paul worked as a tentmaker, a church planter, and an author. His purpose never changed, but his work certainly did. Instead of searching for another job, we may simply need to choose a different attitude or a new point of view about the job we already have. Envision Jesus standing in the midst of your workplace as your *real* boss and see how your perspective changes.

- *God uses coworkers to teach me people skills.* Cooperation, fairness, flexibility, humility, and patience are relationship skills of a successful worker. Stress comes when we stray from the guidelines God gives us for serving others. Our workplace is not only one of our God-ordained mission fields, it is a classroom for learning to love the unlovable, forgiving the unforgivable, and, in short, being "God with skin on."

- *God uses my work to teach me how to serve.* The way we serve God is by serving others. God wants us to grow spiritually at work by becoming a servant to those with whom we work. It's easy to serve those who sit beside us in church each Sunday, but a real servant looks for ways to serve coworkers. Our goal should be to accept others unconditionally, encourage others continually, forgive others freely, and help others willingly—in other words, to have His heart of service.

- *God uses my work to teach me responsibility.* Meeting deadlines, completing assigned tasks with excellence, showing respect for coworkers (even the abrasive ones), working without supervision are all valuable life lessons learned on the job. When we try to cut corners, stress steps in and wreaks havoc in our attitude about work.

Attitudes never sit still. They constantly move and change. An attitude is a pattern of thinking, a filter through which we view life. We can choose to be honest about our attitude at work and we can choose to change our attitude about work, but most importantly we can choose to pray for God's attitude about work. When we can't change our attitude, the One who lives in us can give us His. Exchanging our attitude for God's attitude always eliminates stress.

Application steps:

Consider the ways God uses your job to teach you the valuable life lessons listed below. List specific work circumstances and the lessons you learned in each one. Examine your attitude about your work for any changes that need to be made. Record those changes below.

- God uses my work to teach me responsibility. _____

_____

_____

- God uses people at work to teach me about relationships.

_____

_____

- God uses my work to teach me how to serve. _____

_____

_____

Memory verse:

A man can do nothing better than to eat and drink and find satisfaction in his work (Ecclesiastes 2:24).

Reflection points:

Do the people I work with see Christ in me? Do they even know I am a Christian? What changes do I need to make in order to show God's love to my coworkers?

Power verses:

Nothing you do in the Lord's service is ever useless (1 Corinthians 15:58 GNT).

Work hard and cheerfully at all you do, just as though you were working for the Lord...remembering it is the Lord Christ who is going to pay you...He is the one you are really working for (Colossians 3:23-24 TLB).

My heart took delight in all my work (Ecclesiastes 2:10).

One new truth: _____

_____

_____

My prayer for today:

Lord, thank You for Your provision through my job. I praise You for the opportunity to serve You and others through my work. Help me to see those in need and reach out to them in Your name. Amen.

Chapter Five: Expect Some Valleys

Key verses:

> You, Lord, give true peace. You give peace to those who depend on you. You give peace to those who trust you. So, trust the Lord always. Trust the Lord because he is our Rock forever (Isaiah 26:3-4 ICB).

Key truths:

According to the National Institute of Mental Health, approximately 40 million Americans suffer from some form of anxiety disorder, including panic disorder, obsessive-compulsive disorder, post-traumatic stress disorder, phobias, and generalized anxiety disorder. In fact, many health organizations and physicians now believe that 80 to 90 percent of all disease is stress related.

A reporter was interviewing a widow who had successfully raised a very large family. In addition to six children of her own, she had adopted twelve other youngsters, and through it all, she had maintained stability and an air of confidence. When asked the secret of her outstanding accomplishment, her answer to the newsman was quite surprising. She said, "I manage so well because I'm in a partnership!" "What do you mean?" he inquired. The woman replied, "Many years ago I said, 'Lord, I'll do the work and You do the worrying.' I've had peace ever since."

We all long for an inner calm—especially in the valleys of life. We all want, pray for, and pursue peace. Many believe that peace is the absence of valleys, trials, and problems. In reality, peace is a calm confidence even in the midst of the valley. That kind of peace is only found in God. When we enter into a personal relationship with Jesus Christ, we enter into true peace.

Since we have been made right with God by our faith, we

have peace with God. This happened through our Lord Jesus Christ (Romans 5:1 NCV).

We will experience peace when we are willing to move away from our sin toward the Prince of Peace, Jesus Christ, in a personal relationship. When John Paton was translating the Bible for a South Seas island tribe, he discovered they had no word for "peace." One day a native who had been running hard came to the missionary's house, flopped down into a large chair, and said, "It's good to rest my whole weight on this chair." Paton thought for a minute and said, "I'll translate "peace" as the result of resting one's whole weight on God." Many things weigh us down, but all of them can and must be given to God in order to experience peace. Allowing God to carry the weight of worry, the burden of anxiety, and the penalty of every sin will bring peace and allow us to escape the deadly trap of stress.

Application steps:

- Recognize God as the only source of true peace.
- Completely surrender your valley to God.
- Confess any known sin and turn from it.
- Choose to rest in Him.

Memory verse:

> We can say with confidence, "The Lord is my helper; I will not be afraid. What can man do to me?" (Hebrews 13:6).

Reflection points:

- I have tried to find peace in _____.

- The valley I am facing today is _____

  My response to this valley has been _____

  _____.

- Right now, I turn it all over to God and choose to rest in Him, Shepherd of my every valley. _____

_____

_____

Power verses:

Consider it pure joy, my brothers, whenever you face trials of many kinds, because you know that the testing of your faith develops perseverance. Perseverance must finish its work so that you may be mature and complete, not lacking anything. If any of you lacks wisdom, he should ask God, who gives generously to all without finding fault, and it will be given to him (James 1:2-5).

Give thanks in all circumstances, for this is God's will for you in Christ Jesus (1 Thessalonians 5:18).

I leave you peace; my peace I give you. I do not give it to you as the world does. So don't let your hearts be troubled or afraid (John 14:27 NCV).

One new truth: _____

_____

_____

My prayer for today:

Lord, it seems that anxiety and doubt are my constant companions. This valley seems so deep and so dark. By faith, I choose to trust You, my Shepherd. I am so tired, Father. Will You please carry me? I can't see what is ahead. Will You please guide me? I am discouraged and ready to quit. Will You please be my strength? I love You and want to please You with my life. Empower me to be all You created me to be. Amen.

Chapter Six: Manage Your Fears

Key verse:

> God has not given us a spirit of fear, but of power and of love and of a sound mind (2 Timothy 1:7 NKJV).

Key truths:

We do a lot of laundry at the Southerland house. There always seems to be a load in the washer that needs to go in the dryer, a load in the dryer that needs to be folded, and a load of dirty laundry waiting to begin the process all over again. Our washer and dryer have numerous settings for everything from hand washables and fine delicates to cotton and permanent press. After a few loads that yielded pink male underwear and sweaters shrunk to fit Barbie dolls, we decided to wash everything on one setting. Heaven help the man, woman, or child who dares to change that setting.

When a life crisis comes, we generally have an automatic setting of fear and anxiety. The good news is that we can change that setting to peace and joy. How? By counting on God.

1. *Count on God to be with you.* We battle stress every day, but God is faithful and we can count on Him to be with us. Worry is trying to fix tomorrow's problems with today's resources. God gives grace in daily doses.

> When you go through deep waters and great trouble, I will be with you. When you go through rivers of difficulty, you will not drown! When you walk through the fire of oppression, you will not be burned up; the flames will not consume you (Isaiah 43:2 NLT).

2. *Count on God for direction.* Life can easily spin out of control in a whirlwind of confusion. God offers clear direction and guidance through His Word, through His people, and through the Holy Spirit.

I will guide you along the best pathway for your life. I will
advise you and watch over you (Psalm 32:8 NLT).

3. *Count on God for provision.* God goes before us in every area of
life. Nothing that happens to us will ever surprise Him. We must
be careful to stay away from scenario sickness of what-if. There
are no what-ifs when we choose to trust God for every need.

I will provide their needs before they ask. I will help them
while they are still asking for help (Isaiah 65:24 NCV).

4. *Count on God for protection.* God will fight for us when we are
attacked. When we follow His agenda, God fights for us, but
when we follow our agenda, we are on our own.

The LORD will fight for you; you need only to be still
(Exodus 14:14).

I recently saw a bumper sticker that read, "If God is your Co-
pilot, switch seats!" We have good reason to be afraid when we are
in control. Fear feeds stress. Stress thrives in an atmosphere of fear
and doubt when our hand is on the steering wheel of life. We need
to move over, surrender control to God, and find the peace waiting
in His hand.

Application steps:

Make a list of your fears. Surrender each one to the loving control of God as you pray, "I will fear no evil, for You are with me."
Burn the list as an offering of praise and thanksgiving to God's
perfect peace enthroned in your life.

Memory verse:

God is our refuge and strength, an ever-present help in
trouble (Psalm 46:1).

Reflection points:

What fears am I facing today? _____

_____

What step(s) do I need to take in order to find victory over those

fears? _____

_____

Power verses:

> Because you are my help, I sing in the shadow of your wings.
> My soul clings to you; your right hand upholds me
> (Psalm 63:7-8).

> I will lead the blind by ways they have not known, along
> unfamiliar paths I will guide them; I will turn the darkness
> into light before them and make the rough places smooth.
> These are the things I will do; I will not forsake them
> (Isaiah 42:16).

> Set me free from my prison, that I may praise your name
> (Psalm 142:7).

One new truth: _____

_____

_____

My prayer for today:

Father, my heart is filled with fear. It seems as though I am drowning in the uncertainties of my life. Lord, help me to surrender my fears to You. Strengthen me to face each one and walk through it, knowing that You are with me. I choose to trust You and doubt my fears. I choose against stress and for peace. I choose You, Lord. Amen.

Chapter Seven: Celebrate the Battle

Key verses:

> Do not be anxious about anything, but in everything, by prayer and petition, with thanksgiving, present your requests to God. And the peace of God, which transcends all understanding, will guard your hearts and your minds in Christ Jesus (Philippians 4:6-7).

Key truths:

Someone recently gave me a refrigerator magnet that said, "I know God promises to never give me more than I can handle. But sometimes, I just wish He didn't trust me so much." When trials come and life seems hard, we plead with God to deliver us *from* the problem when many times His plan is to deliver us *in* the problem. Praise does not depend upon an understanding of the circumstance or trial. Praise depends upon faith in the God of that circumstance or trial.

As humans, we will never fully understand God—this side of heaven. He is holy and without blemish. He is all powerful and omniscient. He is the Creator of the universe and yet lives in you and me. He is the only true, living God. We may understand some of His ways and comprehend the reasoning behind some of His plans. We may even come to the place of knowing Him on what we call an intimate level, but a full understanding of God is reserved for heaven. Until then, we walk by faith, not by sight. We praise Him in the darkness, knowing that the light is just ahead. We trust Him for things we cannot see and praise Him in the valleys. Honestly, the thought of serving and relying on a God I don't fully understand is not a reassuring thought.

Most people who know me well would describe me as a strong

person, someone who can usually handle what life holds. I thought the same thing until I found myself a powerless prisoner of the darkness as I battled clinical depression. It took me two long years to climb out of that pit, and not a day goes by that I'm not reminded of that wonderful, horrible time. One of the many lessons I learned from my "pit experience" was that I cannot depend upon my own strength or my fickle emotions. God often asked me to praise Him when, as far as I could tell, there wasn't a whole lot to praise Him for. I didn't *feel* like praising Him. I began to understand that praise is not a feeling but a choice, a step of obedience taken without the assurance of a changed circumstance or the elimination of a trial. Praise focuses on God, not the circumstance, and fixes its gaze upon God's truth and God's character instead of the trial at hand or the one just ahead. That's why we can celebrate the battle before it begins. The outcome is neither our responsibility nor our goal. Praise begins and ends with faith in the very nature, personality, and integrity of God...and that reality never changes.

No matter what lies ahead, God is faithful. No matter how hot the fiery trial may be, He will deliver us. No matter what man says or does, He loves and accepts us. So praise God. Thank Him today for every victory tomorrow holds. Celebrate—knowing the battle belongs to Him and because of that single truth, victory is certain.

Application steps:

Begin your "Joy Journal" by recording the daily blessings God gives you each day. Remember to add small miracles as well as large ones. At the end of the week, have a private praise service—just you and God. Thank Him for His presence and power at work in your life.

Memory verse:

> And the peace of God, which transcends all understanding, will guard your hearts and your minds in Christ Jesus (Philippians 4:7).

Reflection points:

- When I hear the word "praise," what comes to my mind?
- Do I really believe my life can bring God pleasure?
- After reading Psalm 139, how do I think God sees me?
- What are the sources of discouragement in my life?
- What steps do I need to take to eliminate those sources?

Power verses:

> O Jehovah come and bless us!...Satisfy us in our earliest youth with your loving-kindness giving us constant joy to the end of our lives (Psalm 90:13-14 TLB).

> Enter his gates with thanksgiving; go into his courts with praise. Give thanks to him and bless his name. For the LORD is good. His unfailing love continues forever, and his faithfulness continues to each generation (Psalm 100:4-5 NLT).

> Let them give thanks to the LORD for his love and for the miracles he does for people (Psalm 107:8 ICB).

One new truth: _____

_____

_____

My prayer for today:

Father, I praise You today for all that You have done in my life. You are faithful even when I am faithless. Your love pursues me even when I am unlovable. Your forgiveness covers my sin and frees me from its penalty. Lord, teach me to praise You. Help me to see and understand the power of praising You in my life. I want to bring You pleasure, Father. I praise You for Your love and faithfulness to me. Your presence in my life changes everything, empowering me to live each moment of every day, content in knowing You are in control. As I face today, Lord, remind me that no matter what happens, I can praise You. Amen.

Chapter Eight: Count on Grace

Key verses:

> I waited patiently for the LORD; he turned to me and heard my cry. He lifted me out of the slimy pit, out of the mud and mire; he set my feet on a rock and gave me a firm place to stand. He put a new song in my mouth, a hymn of praise to our God. Many will see and fear and put their trust in the LORD (Psalm 40:1-3).

Key truths:

There are few certainties in this world. God is one. His promises are true and we can wholly trust Him to keep His Word and to do exactly what He promises to do. In the verses above, God promises to free us from the pits of life, to direct and restore us—and He invites us to join Him in kingdom work. In other words, He promises grace for the journey.

Ah, there is that word again—grace. I am amazed when I think about the price tag dangling from the gift of grace. Grace cost God His Son and Jesus His very life. When Jesus came to earth as man, He came as a living, fleshed-out illustration of grace. Grace allows us to take a long look at life, keeping our glance on circumstances and our gaze on the Lord of the circumstances. Grace pursues us and loves us, even when we run and reject God's love. Grace heals the wounded heart and saves the broken soul. God is drawn to brokenness.

What an amazing truth, that God turns first to the broken. Psalm 40:1 says, "He turned to me." Notice this passage doesn't say that David, the author, turned to God. I don't think David *could* turn to God. Knowing the desire of David's heart and understanding his weakness, God heard his cry and turned to David just the way He will hear your cry and turn to you.

During the darkest hours of my battle with clinical depression, I continually questioned God, flinging my anger at Him like a spear. My heart and soul were filled with fear and confusion instead of faith and trust. Yet He never turned away from me. He knew every tear I cried, and out of those tears and brokenness has come the most effective and powerful chapter of my life. I have discovered that the more we are broken, the more we are used—because of grace.

You can count on God. You can credit His grace to your account. We are trophies of God's grace and we can count on Him.

Application steps:

Recognize the truth that the only source of true forgiveness and complete restoration is God. What areas of your life need His restoration power? What steps do you need to take in order for God to work in your life? List each step in your journal. Pray about each step and then take action. Remember, God is more interested in what you do than what you know. Step out in faith. He will meet you there.

Memory verse:

The LORD replied, "If you return to me, I will restore you so you can continue to serve me" (Jeremiah 15:19 NLT).

Reflection points:

Mercy is when we don't get what we deserve. Justice is when we get what we do deserve, but grace is when we get what we do not deserve. Think about these statements and compare them to your own definition of grace. Have there been specific times when you sensed the work of grace in your life? Reflect on those times. Record them in your journal.

Power verses:

I will lead the blind by ways they have not known, along

unfamiliar paths I will guide them; I will turn the darkness into light before them and make the rough places smooth. These are the things I will do; I will not forsake them (Isaiah 42:6).

Then they cried to the LORD in their trouble, and he saved them from their distress. He brought them out of darkness and the deepest gloom and broke away their chains (Psalm 107:13-14).

You have seen me tossing and turning through the night. You have collected all my tears and preserved them in your bottle! You have recorded every one in your book (Psalm 56:8 TLB).

Oh, what a wonderful God we have! How great are his riches and wisdom and knowledge! How impossible it is for us to understand his decisions and his methods! (Romans 11:33 NLT).

One new truth: _____

_____

_____

My prayer for today:

Father, I celebrate the truth that You are a God of grace and that You love me unconditionally. Help me to see Your hand of grace at work in my life. I surrender myself to You and ask that You shape and form me into the image of Your Son, Jesus. I want to be like Him, Lord. Amen.

Chapter Nine: Take the Long Look

Key verse:

Why am I so sad? Why am I so upset? I should put my hope in God. I should keep praising him, my Savior and my God (Psalm 42:11 ICB).

Key truths:

I am famous for my "brown thumb." Even though we have moved several times over the years, changing climates, states, neighborhoods, and soil conditions, nothing has altered the fact that if I touch any living plant, its chances for survival are slim. My husband has fared no better in his numerous attempts to plant trees and flowers. I fear that "brown thumb" disease is contagious. There is more. I see undeniable evidence that this gardening malady is hereditary. My son, bless his heart, has tried to rescue wilted flower after crispy plant from his mother's clutches. Like his father, nearly every tree or flower planted by Jered has died. But there is hope! My daughter, Danna, is not only able to keep living plants alive for an impressive amount of time, she can plant seeds and green things will actually grow! It's amazing to me.

When Danna was in kindergarten, she had a very creative science teacher, Miss Kay, who constantly planned fun activities and projects for the children. Danna loved her and was always talking about what she learned in science class. One day, as I waited for Danna in the carpool line, I spotted her standing by Miss Kay, grinning from ear to ear, jumping up and down as if she simply could not wait for me to get there. As I pulled up, Danna hopped into the car, gave a huge sigh of satisfaction and stretched out her tiny hand, proudly displaying the amazing reason for her enthusiasm—a wadded up paper towel.

Now, I am normally very good at being excited about the things my kids find important, but for the life of me, I could not fathom why Danna would be so thrilled with a crumpled paper towel. "Honey, what is that?" I asked. She looked up at me with sparkling brown eyes and whispered, "Mom, there are seeds in here. Miss Kay gave them to me and I'm gonna plant them and they are gonna grow. Can you believe it?"

Given my morbid experience with seeds, I declined to answer that question but instead, chose to join my daughter in her excitement—until I saw them. Evidently, Danna had been carrying the seeds around all day because when she carefully unfolded the paper towel all I could see was a big mess of broken, mismatched, crushed, and crumbled seeds. Looking into the eager eyes of my daughter, I said, "Honey, if these seeds don't grow for some reason, remember that we can go to the store and buy some new ones." Clutching the seeds tightly to her heart and safely out of my reach, Danna said, "Mama, they have to grow 'cause I prayed and asked God to please make them grow and He said He would!"

I began planning our trip to the gardening center.

Danna was silent all the way home, but when we pulled into our driveway, she jumped out of the car and darted into the house, leaving her doubting mother behind. Moments later, she ran back outside with a small paper cup in her hand. I watched as she scooped up dirt from the front flower bed and marched confidently back into the house. I followed her, moaning my silent complaint. "Father, do You realize that Your reputation is on the line here? Why did she have to pick *that* particular flower bed, the one we filled with rocks because nothing, not even weeds, will grow there?" Once again, I tried to reason with my daughter. "Honey, why don't we just buy some new seeds?" Ignoring my faithless question and attitude, Danna stuffed the broken seeds down into the cup, marched to the kitchen sink and, placing the cup under the faucet, turned the water on full blast. Just as fast as the seeds and dirt spilled over the edge of the cup into the sink, Danna scooped them up and poked them back in, all the way to the bottom of the cup so they wouldn't escape. "Miss Kay says they have to have sunshine to grow." With this announcement, she placed her soggy cup of broken, mismatched seeds in worthless dirt on the kitchen windowsill that looks out over our screened-in porch; a place purposely designed to receive no sunlight at all. By this time, I knew that my words were falling on deaf ears and decided to let God handle this one.

Several days later, I was standing at the kitchen sink preparing dinner when I glanced out on the porch to see my daughter's faith on spectacular display. A small paper cup filled with green sprouts confronted my doubting heart. I could not believe my eyes. Dropping the potatoes in the sink, I literally ran to Danna's room shouting, "Danna! Danna! Your seeds are growing!" I found her calmly playing Chutes and Ladders with Danielle, her best friend. "Danna, did you hear me? Your seeds are growing!" A brief glance and knowing smile from Danna said it all. "That's neat, Mom. I knew they would." She and Danielle resumed their game, leaving me to gaze in awe and wonder at the faith of my child who dared, against all odds, to believe.

You may be hopeless, clinging to the broken and mismatched remnants of your life, wondering how you can go on. Whispers of the enemy may creep into your heart, soul, and mind, taunting you with the lie that you are just too dirty and broken for God to love or use. Nothing you do can change that reality so you might as well give up, throwing your life away.

Nothing could be further from the truth, my friend. Never underestimate the power of one, tiny broken seed. Placed in the right hands, it will surely grow into an expression of God's beauty for all to see.

Application steps:

In order to live a life filled with hope, we must make several choices:

• Choose faith over doubt.

- Choose to believe God's Word over man's wisdom.
- Choose to stand firm when the storms come.
- Choose to count on God's holiness instead of our efforts.

Memory verse:

The sacrifice you want is a broken spirit. A broken and repentant heart, O God, you will not despise (Psalm 51:17 NLT).

Reflection points:

What areas of my life are filled with doubt instead of hope? How can I walk by faith in these areas? How can I use God's Word to strengthen my faith and bring hope?

Power verses:

Be joyful because you have hope. Be patient when trouble comes. Pray at all times (Romans 12:12 ICB).

Christ in you, the hope of glory (Colossians 1:27 NASB).

It is for this we labor and strive, because we have fixed our hope on the living God, who is the Savior of all men, especially of believers (1 Timothy 4:10).

One new truth: _____

_____

_____

My prayer for today:

Lord, I confess that when life is hard, I tend to lose hope. I want my hope to be in You, Father. I want to walk in faith and in Your will for my life. I am so tired of being defeated. Please show me how to walk in obedience, and by doing so, to walk in hope. Amen.

Journey Ministry

○ ○ ○

As with any journey, there are unseen detours, unexpected stops, and surprising turns in the road—and priceless treasures to be found along the way. I want to encourage you and walk with you, knowing God has gone before us to order each step and keep His eye on every storm.

That's right—no matter where the journey leads, God is there. Rest assured that He is Lord of every mountain, Shepherd of every valley, Friend of every wounded heart...and He loves you.

Mary

Mary Southerland is a pastor's wife, the mother of two, an author, and an international speaker. A dynamic communicator, Mary delivers a powerful message that changes lives. She will make you laugh, cry, and walk away thirsting for more. Through warmth, humor, transparency, and solid biblical teaching, she leads women to discover the powerful truth of God's Word and motivates them to apply it in their daily lives. She is also the founder of Journey Ministry, a teaching ministry dedicated to equipping every woman for her unique journey to the heart of God.

Mary is available to speak for conferences,
retreats, and women's events:

Website: www.marysoutherland.com
E-mail: journeyfriends@cs.com
Phone: 704-843-2934

About Ellen and Sally

Ellen Briggs, Food Consultant, has spent most of her career in sales and marketing in the media, advertising, and natural foods industries. She is a food expert, focusing on the value of making better food choices. Learn more about how to take the stress out of feeding your family in her articles, seminars, speaking engagements, and media appearances. Ellen is a mother of two, grandmother of three, and the coauthor of *Are Your Kids Running on Empty?* and *Mom, I'm Hungry, What's for Dinner?*

www.betterfoodchoices.com

○ ○ ○

Sally Byrd, N.D., LMBT, is a board-certified and licensed naturopath, as well as a licensed body worker. With more than 25 years as a professional in the natural foods industry, she has amassed a wealth of knowledge in the field of nutrition. Her lifetime commitment to health education has been spread across the United States and the Caribbean through her seminars. Sally is a mother of two and the coauthor of *Are Your Kids Running on Empty?* and *Mom, I'm Hungry. What's for Dinner?*

www.betterfoodchoices.com

Also by Mary Southerland

EXPERIENCING GOD'S POWER IN YOUR MINISTRY
Success and Survival for Every Woman Who Serves God

Going the Distance—or Going to Pieces?

As a Bible study leader, women's ministry director, church staffer, pastor's wife, or pastor, you have unique spiritual and day-to-day needs. Novice or veteran, here you'll find refreshment, inspiration, and motivation to go the distance in loving and serving others.

Straightforward and supportive, Mary Southerland lines out key biblical habits that will bring practical, energizing benefits in your life and help you to

- *allow God to unleash His power* in tough relationships and circumstances
- *recognize who you really are*—a woman pursued and chosen by God
- *have the courage to openly embrace transition* and not just stay comfortable
- *stand firm in the storms,* rather than give up
- *aim for greatness*—because you're serving a great God

In each chapter, Mary adds a study section and an in-the-trenches interview or story from a woman in ministry. All this adds up to a powerful resource that will encourage you to keep running the race and to celebrate what God is doing through you and others.

Great for personal, staff, and curriculum use

"Women in ministry will be drawn to Mary's humor, warmth, and transparency—and her 'tell it like it is' approach to the joys and struggles of ministry life."
—**Kay Warren,** wife of Rick Warren, pastor, Saddleback Church

HARVEST HOUSE
PUBLISHERS

Also by
Mary Southerland

SANDPAPER PEOPLE
Dealing with the Ones Who Rub You the Wrong Way

"God, why did You put these problem people in my life?"

The unwanted intrusion of a nosy neighbor...the exasperating call from your least favorite coworker...the latest mess-up by the relative who doesn't seem to want to change...

If you've run out of ideas for handling your difficult relationships, perhaps it's time to try a fresh approach. Working from a toolbox full of anecdotes and humor, Mary Southerland presents action principles for relating to the abrasive people in your life, such as...

recognizing their worth

knowing when to confront

refusing to walk away

Chapter-by-chapter questions, applications, and journaling suggestions will help you recognize your own sandpaper tendencies and see your sandpaper people for what they are: opportunities from God to grow—while being transformed in the process.

HARVEST HOUSE
PUBLISHERS

Bible Credits